HEY, KIDS, WATCH THIS

GO **BEYOND** AGING WELL

YOU CAN BE A PERSON IN CRESCENDO—NO MATTER HOW OLD YOU ARE OR WHAT HAPPENS

NIKKI HANNA

Published by Patina Publishing
727 S. Norfolk Avenue
Tulsa, Oklahoma 74120
neqhanna@sbcglobal.net
www.nikkihanna.com

IBSN: 978-0-9828726-2-8

Library of Congress LCCN: 2015916321

Manufactured in The United States of America

Photography: Stephen Michaels, Tulsa, Oklahoma

Contributors: Lhonda Harris, Pillars of Sloth,
Participants in Lifelong Learning Programs

DEDICATION

To Ron Mainer and Peggy Jones,
who didn't live to be old.

To Mom and Dad, who did.

AUTHOR'S NOTE:

I accidentally wrote this book. While developing handouts for a seminar on *Aging Beyond Well* for a university's lifelong learning program, I combined the handout materials into one computer file. After doing so, it occurred to me the file could easily be made into a book. So I designed a cover, tacked on a Table of Contents, rounded out the material, massaged it a bit, and this happened: *Hey, Kids, Watch This*. I hope you enjoy my accidental book and that you steal some of its shine. . .Nikki Hanna

If you are over fifty, this is your time,
and it can be your best time.

It is possible you have one third of your
life left to live. That's a lot of time to coast.

TABLE OF CONTENTS

INTRODUCTION

On his first day in first grade, a little boy, who had gone to kindergarten in the mornings the previous year, loaded up his backpack at noon. His teacher asked, "What are you doing, Toby?" He responded, "Getting ready to go home." She explained, "Oh no, Toby, in first grade you go to school all day." Toby sat thoughtfully for a moment, arms crossed, lips pursed. Finally, he asked, "Well, who signed me up for this?"

If you are in the last trimester of life, you can relate to this question. Transitioning into retirement and dealing with the complications of aging generate a plethora of issues, including a sense of being disenfranchised. You wonder how to matter going forward. The truth is, you *can* remain relevant, perhaps more so than ever before. It is possible your best days have not happened yet.

Because so much is written about how to age well, this book might be anticipated as being rich with old ideas dressed up in new clothes. However, the perspectives introduced herein bridge the gap between acceptance of life unfolding and aging in a way that promotes bliss. Strategies are introduced that take aging to a level that enhances the lives of others, which is the path to relevance.

As the author, my wish is that this book emboldens and entertains you. I hope your enthusiasm for life is enhanced, your sense of gratefulness enriched, and your awareness of purpose embellished.

Most of all, I hope you consider yourself on the sweet side of sixty—a person in crescendo.

I facilitate workshops in university lifelong learning programs where participants range in age from fifty-five to ninety-something. I initially hesitated to take on that role over concern my age would become the most important thing about me. Then it occurred to me it was, and that was okay. My age is my most valuable asset.

As I moved *beyond* just aging well to aging with bravado, I grew brave and enthusiastic about sharing my aging experiences and appreciating those of others. I became so optimistic about the prospect of turning seventy that I named my sixty-ninth birthday party my *Pushing Seventy Party*. I liked the sound of *seventy*. I couldn't wait to say, "I'm seventy, and I haven't even peaked yet."

At seventy, I'm not an expert on what it is like to be older than I am. I can only imagine with the naiveté of a rookie what aging past seventy is like. Fortunately, older participants in lifelong learning workshops have generously shared their aging exploits, some of which are incorporated in this book. They are my inspiration. I have learned more from them than they have from me. If I get preachy at times, it is their voice coming through.

Most participants in these programs display shining faces, twinkling eyes, and eager expressions. Their sparkle has nothing to do with age, the condition of their bodies, or the consequences of their lives. It has to do with how they choose to experience life. Nothing slows their roll. As seekers, they go *beyond* aging well and display a zest for life. They glow.

A person can begrudge aging or embrace it. Rather than being haunted by the stereotype of aging, it is possible to reframe the process and become a beacon. For those who feel they are disappearing—becoming less relevant—this book suggests a roadmap for a journey from being invisible to mattering. A bold shift in core assumptions proposed herein spurs readers to discover the best part of their older selves.

Legacy is created by how a person ages. The remarkable thing about legacy is that it is forever. It flows through generations. Many people age well, but aging in a way that is a gift to others is going *beyond* well. By doing so, you become a proper ancestor. This may be the most important thing you do in your lifetime, and how to do it is what this book is about.

Those who care about you want you to be okay—need you to be okay. When you are okay to the end—no matter what happens—you soften their worlds and give them peace. This fosters a splendid aging experience, a good goodbye, and a grand and enduring legacy.

Faltering is inherent in the process of aging *beyond* well because challenges are severe. You look into a mirror and conclude your face resembles an unfortunate crochet project. Your hair takes on the attributes of straw. Your knees look like a soufflé. You discover fat in places so peculiar that you feel punked. Your stomach wiggles like Jello. Body parts move around (downward mostly). The shock factor when discovering a chin whisker is similar to that of seeing a hand stick up out of a grave. Your magnetic bracelet is a nuisance because it is so powerful it sticks to the refrigerator. When asked how you are doing, the best you can say is, "I'm *mostly* okay." Nevertheless, you get to choose whether to be a winner or a victim.

This is true as long as you have control over the process of aging. If you live long enough, it is likely that, on some level, control will be lost. Even in that circumstance, though, anticipating and preparing for such a contingency diminishes its influence. It is possible to set up your affairs so others are at peace with whatever happens to you. The alternative is to ignore unfortunate possibilities, do nothing, and leave those you are supposed to care about most to suffer the aftermath of your inaction.

This book goes to the heart of tough issues and confronts the unvarnished truth: The inevitable conclusion of this final phase of life (I'll just say it outright) is death. If you choose to ignore that reality or deceive yourself into viewing death as an option, as many people do (unconsciously), observations of what is happening to peers will telegraph haunting reminders.

When it comes to aging, everyone is afraid on the inside, but growing old is the universe showing off. You can orchestrate your aging experience—not as a burden to those you love—but as a gift. Although anxiety lurks, the body aches, and losses are unrelenting, personal triumph is possible. By aging well, you hum. By going *beyond* aging well, you sing. Construct your experience so you sing like an opera star. Go ahead. Do it. Sing.

This is your time, and it can be your best time.

GETTING STARTED

Why do some people do growing old poorly? Why are precious years wasted when they hold so much potential? Do older people realize how much they influence the futures of others by how they age? The goal of the *"beyond* aging well concept" is to contemplate these questions and to expose flawed stereotypes, introduce fresh perspectives, reveal possibilities, and inspire a robust third trimester of life. To this end, the objectives of this book are:

-To understand the concept of aging *beyond* well and how burdens are lifted for others when a person does so.

-To show how legacy is created by how a person ages and to reveal the power of legacy as a forever gift.

-To demonstrate how to choose a winner mentality over a victim one—no matter what happens.

-To encourage aging with passion and purpose and to show how to find bliss.

To understand aging issues, it helps to appreciate the expansive diversity of the over-fifty population. Grouping all older people together in the category of *seniors* is equivalent to putting a kindergartner into a class with people in their forties who are going through a midlife crisis. Only under limited circumstances is it appropriate to view seniors as a homogeneous group. Variances exist in health, vitality, interests, political views, social positions, religious affiliations, support systems, working status, and financial circumstances. Of particular note is the divide between pre-retirement persons in their fifties and those in their sixties. That is a great divide.

Each decade has delivered its own watershed experiences—wars, crises, social pressures, and economic challenges—that shape perspectives. Depending on their age, groups of older people view the world differently.

Additionally, some older people have parents, spouses, children, and grandchildren, while others do not. Quite a number are seekers. Others stopped learning years ago. Some are downsizing and getting rid of things. Others collect and hold on to possessions with a vengeance. Some are fashionistas while others still wear high school hairdos. Some enjoy old people jokes. Others are offended by them. Many continue to seek the thrill of romance. Others withdraw.

Some people are in denial. Others are so content they've become almost inert. They spend years just going through the motions of life. In contrast, there are those purposeful folks who make the third trimester of their lives their best time.

All this diversity makes dealing with older people's issues a challenge. To explore these perspectives, this book is tailored for both the workshop setting and for individual reading. At the risk of redundancy, excerpts from other books this author has written are used herein to illustrate key points and, in some cases, to entertain. The names used in all stories are not real.

The target audience for this material is people over fifty and those who care about them. To facilitate the ability to construct a purposeful aging experience, the following format is incorporated in each chapter:

Overview - introduces concepts and stories
Quotes* - provoke thought
Questions - stimulate discussion
Closing Comments - encourage action

(*Many quotes are not sourced because they come from anonymous participants in lifelong learning workshops or from the author.)

In spite of the uplifting nature of this book, it is not a Pollyanna portrayal of growing old. Tough issues are addressed directly and candidly. Real and practical alternatives for resolving problems are proposed. Coping strategies that soften harsh realities and provide heavy doses of hope and peace are introduced.

Dedicated to lifting the spirits of those facing aging, *Hey, Kids, Watch This* encourages readers to embrace the last trimester of life as encore years—better than the original show. It demonstrates how to be a proper ancestor and how to accomplish the ultimate achievement—a splendid, enduring legacy.

*Aging is not so much a matter of the body
as it is a matter of the mind.*

I was in a foul mood at my senior line dancing class and contemplated leaving at the break. Then I noticed a woman in a wheelchair wistfully watching the dancers. A sense of my ungratefulness slammed into me—hard. I decided to stay. The music seemed more vibrant, my dancer compadres more precious, and my world more remarkable. I danced my heart out.

Chapter 1

WHY "BEYOND" AGING WELL?

Growing old is a privilege not everyone gets.

"I love growing old," said no one ever. That doesn't mean you are dancing on the deck of the Titanic. There is a difference between bent and broken. Going *beyond* aging well means leading a robust third trimester of life. It is the path to mattering, one that creates a fabulous legacy. This is no little thing because legacies are forever.

Mattering softens the haunting dread of being old and transforms life into something insanely wonderful. Your value becomes less about what extraordinary adventures you experienced in the past and more about what you are doing now.

Divorced, broke, and starting over, Tina Turner performed in a small Tulsa nightclub years ago. She worked for practically nothing to pay off debts incurred during her marriage. My children and I scored front row seats.

Tina hit the stage in a flurry of blazing glory after a musical crescendo worthy of Elvis. She was frigging fabulous, bumping and gyrating to the pounding music in a sequined minidress loaded with fringe, high heels typical of a hooker, and a wildly flailing ponytail on top of her head reminiscent of a Tasmanian cannibal. A sonic boom of energy with the potential to frighten small children and stir the souls of men, she exuded mojo squared.

I expected the strut and sass, the fire. In contrast, my children, wide-eyed and open-mouthed, were stunned—and mesmerized. My preadolescent son spent a good part of the evening making a valiant effort to peer through the flailing fringe on her upper thigh as his younger sister evolved from a state of dazed shock to one of consummate worship.

Tina was reinventing herself as a single, independent woman. After that performance, there was no doubt where she was headed. This was a woman to be reckoned with. She became my idol that day.

Years later, my daughter was a young woman when Tina made her last tour performance. I got tickets for her and her thirty-something girlfriends who asked, "Who is Tina Turner?" After the performance, they knew who Tina Turner was. She was some kind of crazy wonderful—a magnificent, powerful, jaw-dropping engine of dynamic energy. She was woman, she roared, and she was sixty-something.

No one denies that there are major obstacles to constructing a positive aging experience. Relevance is hard earned. Losses are real and constant. Physical and mental agilities fall by the wayside. Cultural issues, technological advances, medical calamities, and family dynamics complicate the aging process.

Important obligations surface because an older person's well-being is a prerequisite to other people's happiness. It is sad when a person sacrifices all their life for their children and then, in the end, create substantial anguish for them.

No matter what trials are encountered, you can age as a *victim* or a *winner*. In the victim mode, you become a loser. People may feel sorry for you, but that role causes them to dread their own futures. Also, being a victim requires a persecutor. When you place someone in that role, you both lose. The diverse paths of winners and losers produce distinctly different results. To be a proper ancestor, you must choose the winner one.

This is a challenge because physical and mental consequences accumulate into a complex system of redundant complaints and inhibitions that wreak havoc and limit choices. Growing old is dicey and precarious, like snuggling up to an ATM at a casino.

Going from aging well to aging *beyond* well requires stepping outside of denial and facing harsh realities head on. At class reunions, conversations are about colonoscopies, hip replacements, and heart stents. Once trendy people are now wearing elastic waist bands and serviceable shoes cinched with velcro and customized with arch supports. Some are widowed. One or two attendees are ironing only the fronts of their clothes because they are in wheelchairs. A few will not make it to the next reunion.

Cosmetic catastrophes are commonplace— peculiar elbows, thinning hair, disappearing eyebrows, and an ever-expanding midsection. You see a reflection in a window and wonder, *Who is that old person?* Reality hits, and you realize, *It is me.* You hope you look better from the back. You don't.

Perhaps, when it comes to sex, all you can do is run to the end of the chain and bark. Sabotaged by hearing loss, floaters in the eyes, exploding brown spots, earlobe issues that complicate the accessory selection process, and wrinkles, it is clear you are no longer bathing in the fountain of youth. But wrinkles don't hurt, and you are still here. Others are not. A wrinkle is not an existential crisis. Cancer is. Cosmetic changes represent natural aesthetics—evidence of the gift of time.

As all manner of indignities materialize, it is important you find a way to be okay with them. They are life happening, and that's a good thing. When you feel jealous of the young, ask yourself this:

> Would you really want to repeat those younger years of ignorance and foolishness? As bad as aging is, it is better than being a small child chased by a rooster, or a young man who decided to "get this party started" and ended up as a yard ornament on his parent's front lawn, or a young mother who found her infant covered in shit in the crib, or a naive divorcee wrapped in the arms of a man resembling a whisky-induced orangutan, or a woman experiencing a menopausal hot flash in a vehicle without air-conditioning, or an employee working for a boss with the attributes of Attila the Hun, or a man who hits a deer and loads it into a car only to discover it's not dead.

Although the later stage of life is characterized by losses, when one thing is lost, something else is gained. With the loss of youth, comes wisdom. With the loss of appearance, comes freedom, a renewed focus, and even fun. Two sisters who were losing their vision joked that when their eyesight was completely gone, they could give each other makeovers.

Okay. Okay. That's a bad example. There are better ones. When you can't hear so good, you won't hear music so loud it makes your teeth vibrate. At some point you never have to iron anything—ever. Perhaps someday people will cook for you, and you'll never scrape concrete off a casserole dish again. You won't die vacuuming or mowing. Home maintenance becomes someone else's problem. When you cannot drive, you won't have to parallel park ever again.

Each loss is life happening—even dying. At some point, everyone will face the dreaded end of life. We are all terminal. This is heavy-duty stuff. It's hard to imagine anything worse, but the concept of going *beyond* aging well shines a fresh light on the complex circumstances of growing old, even death. Every misfortune is a teachable moment.

By staring aging in the face and reframing it, a person transforms into a state of gratefulness—a blissful, peaceful awareness of the value of still being here. That perspective fosters the courage to embrace the consequences of growing old, good or bad. It inspires a person to value every minute of life happening and to make it count for something.

———————————

When you go down the victim path, you lose, and you take everyone else with you.

I thought growing old would take longer.

Sixty is not the new forty or fifty. It is sixty.

Retirement reminds me of a line in the book "The Kite Runner." I am being "lifted from the certainty of turmoil and dropped into the turmoil of uncertainty."

I found an old journal recently that contained a fair amount of whining, which rather disgusted me. Whining is no longer in my portfolio of behaviors.

When something bad happens, I ask, "What can I do to make it better?" This is my mission. When I am dying, I will do that well—for others. I will help them through it.

I let people dressed for work or mothers with small children ahead of me in lines, allowing the hectic nature of their lives to float past. My life is mellow.

Years ago a doctor gave me a diagnosis, "You have children." Now I have grandchildren. They are like medicine. To them, I'm a friggin' supernova.

The frantic state of the young causes me to appreciate being old. When around a hyped-up young person, I'm tempted to ask if they forgot their medication.

Someone asked June Carter Cash what she was up to. She said, "I'm just trying to matter."

———————————

1. **What messages are your aging experiences sending—victim or winner?**

2. **What messages do you get from our culture?**

3. **What generally accepted perceptions about aging are not true for you?**

4. **How do you deal with the downsides of aging?**

CLOSING COMMENTS:

To create the forever gift of a splendid legacy, explore possibilities. Rather than fearing the future, consider taking on the role of supporting others in their responses to crises, even your own.

If you wear age like a mark of distinction, you won't feel inadequate because of how old you are and end up like George Gobel who said, "I feel like everyone else is a tuxedo and I'm a pair of brown shoes." Don't be that person.

Teeming with wisdom and released from the burdens of parenting, building, and accumulating, the emerging senior generation is finally free to invest in activities that generate joy and resonate into the future. A primary obstacle to accomplishing this is the preconceived notion of what being older is like. To avoid self-limiting perceptions that pull you into acceptance of the mundane, avoid acquiescing to norms and explore the broad spectrum of options available to you as an older person.

Blinded to the range of possibilities available to her, Carol became suicidal. A close friend monitored her closely. Carol had money saved. In a deep discussion with her one day, the friend suggested that before she kill herself Carol could spend some of it—an option that had not occurred to her.

Her friend said, "Do whatever makes you happy. If you plan to die anyway, you have nothing to lose. Spend your money. Do something outrageously indulgent." That sparked an ah-ha moment, and Carol booked a cruise with a Vietnam vet she hardly knew who also needed a dose of hope. After weeks at sea, they returned tanned, renewed, and still single. She redecorated her house, and he bought a boat.

As part of your aging journey, contemplate fresh and novel alternatives. When you are feeling low, consider doing something outrageously self-indulgent. Spend a week at a four-star waterfront hotel in a beach community. Take a grandchild to Paris and chill in sidewalk cafes or take a train across Canada. Buy a new sofa. Move. You don't have money? Paint your bedroom purple. Eat bacon. Or whatever else suits you. Indulge. Better yet, be generous and do something meaningful for someone else. The possibilities are endless.

When something bad happens, ask, "What can I do to help?" This might be as simple as showing strength and perseverance in the face of adversity—being a rock. People may see you as fragile because you are old. What if you surprise them with your resilience and grit? What if you are the one others look to and lean on when life goes badly? What if you are the orienting axis that rallies the troops and holds the family together? What if. . .?

By how you choose to age, you can shift your journey from the depths of despair into the realm of possibilities. Choose the winner role and shine. The following chapters show how to find that magic.

Downsides are simply life happening.
How you respond to them defines your legacy.

Chapter 2

STRIKE A BARGAIN WITH LIFE
You Get It, You Live It Full Out

I don't think of myself as aging.
I think of myself as evolving. . .Deedee Cox

There is power in perception—how you view the world and your place in it. That, in turn, drives behavior. If you view yourself as a victim, you will have no problem finding persecutors and reasons to suffer. If you view yourself as a winner, positive behaviors will follow. Your interpretation of aging has the potential to change everything, not only for yourself, but for others as well. When interpreting aging as evolution and growth rather than decline, you become a beacon. And you inspire others to see their worlds and futures more positively.

A seventy-year-old woman diagnosed with Type 2 diabetes said, "If I had not lived this long, I would not have this disease. I consider myself lucky.

My friends who are gone will never have this experience. I'll deal with it." How she perceived aging inspired this attitude, and it produced behaviors crucial to achieving a vibrant aging experience. Attitude is powerful. A shift in attitude causes behavior to change automatically. For example:

> If a teenage girl is slumping because she thinks she's too tall, nagging her to stop will accomplish nothing. Instead, convince her that being tall gives her the advantage of presence. Point out a wonderful tall woman as a role model. Giving the girl a sense of the value of her height changes her attitude, and she naturally stands tall and proud.

When you send negative messages about growing old, you cause others to dread their futures. You also inflict guilt-laced burdens on them because people who care about you want to save you from the harsh realities of aging. And they cannot. Why would you portray negative perspectives that burden those you care about most? To be a proper role model, you must refuse to be overwhelmed by the formidable challenges swirling around you.

> A psychologist counseled a young boy disturbed over his parents' divorce. The doctor asked, "Tommy, are you

feeling overwhelmed?" The boy lit up. Excitedly, he said, "Yes! Yes! I have too many whelms."

If you are in the third trimester of life, you know how the boy felt. You are in the theater of "too many whelms." It is tempting to embrace the downsides of aging, which you learned to do from society and those going before you who did not do aging well. If you buy into the stereotype that suggests your best times are behind you, and if you coast, you waste your most valuable possession, your ability to influence others in a positive way.

Each generation pioneered remarkable advances. Now it is time to do something else just as remarkable—to redefine aging. To do that, though, you must re-shuffle the deck and shake off old concepts. What is at stake if you do not is not limited to your ability to relish life. It is also your capacity to enhance the lives of those you love.

Some people lie about their age. Lying says you are ashamed of how old you are. Is this silly? So many people never get to be that old. Should you not be proud and grateful instead?

Denial is not a sustainable model, and misrepresenting age fosters missed opportunities. Consider how people would respond if you lied and said, "I'm *fifty* and I run three miles a day," as compared to "I'm *sixty* and I run three miles a day." Which claim has the wow factor?

An online test reveals biological age as compared to chronological age. People take the test hoping to discover their body is biologically younger than their age. They are quick to report the results. This can backfire, though. You may be sixty and discover your biological age is seventy-something.

Denying age does not change anything. Age is what it is. Unfortunately, the older you get, the more negative connotations people attach to it. By not giving in to the temptation to deny the reality of aging and by redefining it as a gift, you project a positive image that inspires.

––––––––––––––

The very thing I dreaded most, being a burden to those I loved, was happening because they worried about me. And I made that happen. Shoot me please.

I look forward to when I'm seventy. My plan is to razzle-dazzle with the life I'm living. Who knows what I'll do at eighty and ninety. I can pull adventure out of a sink hole.

I surround myself with people who fill me up. I am determined to be a positive, upbeat old guy.

I make excuses for aggressive drivers and rude people. Time is their enemy while it is my friend—my ally even.

Aging is not the only cause of a grumpy disposition. Grumpy old people were once grumpy young people.

Keep mum about aches and pains. Sharing them bums out your peers and makes others want to stay away.

I was unable to conjure up good feelings about rug burns from a fall down the stairs rather than from an erotic experience. So rather than complain and lament, I turned my fall into a funny story.

I didn't expect to disappear, to become a voyeur of life rather than a participant in it. And the anger. I didn't anticipate the anger aging would provoke. If I had acted on my thoughts, I would have gone to jail or at least picked up trash along the side of the highway.

I had moxie. Then I got old and lost it. As my three-year-old grandson said about a lost toy, "It is very somewhere." My moxie was "very somewhere." I was desperate to find it. I did, and that changed everything.

Aging produces losses. There was a time when I could beat just about anyone at Pac Man, and I could eat a cinnamon roll the size of a small dog and not gain weight. Those days are gone. But I'm still here.

I amuse my grandson by exploring dreams of what I want to do when I grow up—outrageously magnificent, wondrous things as well as practical, common ones. Then he tells me his dreams, large and small.

I want to be the kind of woman who can make the name Maude cool.

When you are young, you look forward. When you are old, you look backward. When you are in your sixties, you do both. . .Unknown

---

1. **How can changing how you perceive aging automatically change your behavior?**

2. **Are you experiencing too many whelms? If so, how are you responding to them?**

3. **Do you see yourself as having moxie?**

4. **Should you reveal downsides of aging to others?**

5. **How can you change your aging experience to send positive messages and still be authentic?**

6. **How can you redefine aging as evolution?**

7. **What bargain would you strike with life?**

CLOSING COMMENTS:

Cop an attitude—an outrageously positive one. Become a beacon to others. Your gravitas will embellish the lives of peers and of those younger than yourself. Your messages will flow through generations. How you age—or evolve—may be one of the most important and enduring things you ever do. To do aging *beyond* well, you must face the thorny challenge of remaining relevant.

A willful two-year-old girl held her position with her older brother, insisting that if she were to give up her baby doll play and be a pirate, she got to have two swords. Finally, he acquiesced after which she declared "Aaarrgh!" and tore after him, waving both weapons with a vengeance. Her brother ran like a drug dealer on COPS. Seeing this, her dad concluded, *That girl is going to be trouble.*

He was right. Wearing an eye patch and waving her swords, this sweet, gentle little princess, with jewelry and a tutu under her pirate gear, all of a sudden became indisputably relevant, a gal to be reckoned with.

As we get older, we must fight for relevance and attack aging like a pirate with two swords. Striking a bargain with life requires that you remain relevant. It ascribes meaning to your presence and answers the question, "Why am I still here?"

Regardless of what aging dishes out, fight for that relevance, always. Aaarrgh!

Maintaining an upbeat outlook is a challenge. When bombarded with menacing prospects, the *fake it till you make it* tactic can be helpful. If you are bummed and feeling like withdrawing from the world because you are in an unpleasant frame of mind, try pushing ahead with social interactions. Force yourself to be upbeat and playful. Put your focus on making experiences enjoyable for others. Fake it, and you will soon find yourself in a state of enjoyment.

Consider the difference between this outcome and one where you isolate yourself or socialize in a bad mood and bring everyone down. Gaps between negative alternatives and upbeat ones are enormous, and the consequences significantly divergent.

At sixty something, you may have thirty-some years left. That's one-third of a lifetime and a lot of time to waste. You can live this time full out with a sort of *je ne sais quoi*, or you can just go through the motions of life. Once time is wasted, you can't get it back. A positive path not taken represents rejection of your potential. Strike a bargain with life. You get it, you make those years count for something outrageously fantastic.

Don't allow the naiveté of youth
to be replaced by the naiveté of age.

Chapter 3

THE ROAD TO RELEVANCE

At sixty you begin to disappear.

A sense of disappearing as you move into your sixties is pervasive. It creeps in insidiously, eating away at one's sense of self. Dismissiveness is wounding, especially when exhibited by the young. You sacrificed so much for them. They stand on your shoulders. It hurts when they think you don't matter and that your wisdom no longer applies.

Almost three, Hannah was becoming social and sought out people connections wherever she could find them. Sitting in front of two ladies in their seventies at a park concert, she turned around to them and asked, "What are your names?"

Delighted to be asked, Vera replied, "I'm Vera, and this is Florence."

Hannah asked a question people ask her, "How old are you?" She expected the ladies to hold up fingers.

Surprised and tickled by the question, the ladies answered it. Hannah, who could only count to twenty, responded with a cautious "Oh." She turned around in her chair and sat there thoughtfully pondering the mystery of their answers.

Shortly after, she scurried off to dance in the grass to *Reggae Rage,* demonstrating moves that delighted Vera and Florence. Her long blond hair flew wildly with each twist and turn as she gleefully executed amazing moves. She was a blaze of glory—her whole life ahead of her. Later, she said to the ladies as they were leaving, "Nice to meet you."

Not having learned yet that people like Vera and Florence are irrelevant, Hannah was the only person to interact with them at the park that day. To others, such women are in the realm of irrelevance—a stage of life that, in our culture, is viewed by many as insignificant.

In the workplace older employees are frequently devalued. And younger co-workers—hankering for promotions—wish they would leave. Such acts of dismissiveness are not limited to the young, though.

Older people frequently view those older than themselves as irrelevant. Why? Because no one wants to be old. Those the closest to "being old" can be the most prejudicial toward those who are older than themselves. This is because they prefer not to be reminded of where they are headed. They distance themselves from aging like a naughty pet who won't look at his owner. Here are examples of age issues:

It was important to an eighty-six-year-old woman that everyone knew she was younger than another elderly lady in her circle. There was only a six month difference in their ages.

People consider those a decade older than themselves as old until they reach that milestone themselves. Then they view the next age group as old. Oliver Wendell Holmes said, "Old age is fifteen years older than I am."

A man in his seventies at a senior social function complained, "Everyone in here is old." This is as ridiculous as a drunk in a bar complaining, "Everyone in here is drunk."

Our culture promotes mostly unflattering interpretations of aging, but there is another reason older people are considered irrelevant. It is how they behave. Being preoccupied with the past and espousing a litany of complaints turns people off.

Walking the line between being honest and transparent and withholding unpleasant information requires finesse. When a major issue or medical problem surfaces, sharing that misfortune allows others to support your struggle. If you don't include them, they may feel hurt. In general, though, nothing is gained by sharing minor grievances. Doing so is why young people say, "Don't ask an old person how they feel unless you really want to know. They are not going to say, 'Fine.'"

Most older people dislike the *senior* label. It stereotypes them. And it is a rare person who can get excited about the label of septuagenarian or octogenarian. Still, many older people buy into the *senior* stereotype. As a result, self-limiting behavior abounds. In this circumstance, being dismissed by others is accepted as the norm.

Relevance doesn't come easy. You must fight for it, as this old folk tale illustrates:

> Two elderly women, who were members of a nomadic tribe in the polar region, were abandoned. Devoted mothers and grandmothers, these women were loved, but children were starving and caring for the old ladies had become a burden. The tribe wandered off into the frozen tundra in a quest for food, tearfully leaving the women behind in the snowy wilderness.

Realizing their onerous predicament, the women switched into survival mode and surprised themselves with their capabilities. Wisely, they relocated and constructed shelter. Recalling hunting and foraging techniques taught by their fathers years ago, they trapped and fished, eventually amassing a substantial store of food.

Weeks later, the tribe, still ravaged by the harsh winter, stumbled upon them. The old women generously and gleefully shared the rewards of their labors and rescued them all.

At first blush, this tale suggests that the tribe should have valued the women more. However, a deeper interpretation reveals that the women should have valued themselves more. By underestimating their ability to contribute, they became victims dependent on others. Failing to realize what they had to offer, they deprived the tribe of their capabilities. *The old women became relevant, not because of what anyone else did, but because of what they did.*

You can be relevant throughout your aging experience. When you can't take care of yourself anymore, you can be nice to the people taking care of you. Those caring for older people are, no doubt, struggling to provide for their families. How you treat them matters. You can make their day just by the way you light up when they enter your room.

Dismissiveness works both ways. Old people tend to be dismissive of the young, judging them harshly and assuming their energy and fervor are foolish. It is easy to drift into a condescending and critical attitude toward those who display youthful exuberance and who embrace modern trends. Is that the impression you want to have on young people struggling to find their way in the world?

When aging is mastered, compassion flourishes. Mutually respectful people embrace the positives of all age groups. This is a fruitful outcome in contrast to one where groups judge, criticize, and dismiss each other. The close connections inter-generational relationships produce are powerful and uplifting. And, because they model the value of such alliances for future generations, they create legacy.

———————

Aging is a high-pitched noise the young cannot hear.

At age twenty we worry about what others think of us. At age forty, we don't care what they think of us. At age sixty, we discover they haven't been thinking of us at all. . .Ann Landers

I admit to looking down on people older than me. Perhaps it is because I see in them my own future, and I dread it. I prefer to view aging as something happening to someone else.

We should be careful about what we share with the young. They don't care if we are at risk for deep vein thrombosis, or that our testosterone level is low, or that we ever engaged in a panty raid. On second thought, they might find the panty raid entertaining.

My grown daughter said to me one day, "When I was little, I thought you were smart."

When I began relating to my son in an adult-to-adult manner, I stopped judging him. The lectures stopped. I allowed him his own world view. Our differences melted away, and he began valuing my input more.

I still have influence. I convinced my two-year-old granddaughter not to sit and sympathize with her older brother who was in timeout for hitting her.

I tell my grandchildren, "You are as important as the stars." I feel that way about myself, too.

Don't tell young people they can do anything. They can't. Tell them to find their own personal magic—what they were born to do—and to do that.

*We are all connected. There are no others. . .*Ancient Philosopher

*Just by "being" you are enough. . .*Ancient Philosopher

————————

1. What has been your experience with relevance?

2. At what point did you notice the dismissiveness of others? At a certain age? When you retired?

3. Has retirement affected how others relate to you?

4. Are all age groups dismissive to older ones?

5. Are you dismissive of the young? Do you make them feel good? Do you judge them?

6. Should you keep your lips sealed on aches and pains? Does such information turn people off?

7. What can you do to make yourself interesting? Do you keep telling the same old stories over and over again, or are you creating new ones?

8. Are you up on current events?

9. Can technology and social media provide channels for connecting with others?

10. Does asking for assistance keep you connected to others? How do you avoid being a burden?

11. Does relating to grown children in an adult-to-adult manner improve relations?

CLOSING COMMENTS:

You don't care if Beyonce outsells Miley, but your grandchildren do. What you care about is that Mary Ann Faithful is in a hospital in Greece with a broken hip, but your grandchildren don't know who she is. So what? There are many ways to step into the orbit of the young.

It is not necessary to get tattoos or mutilate your body with piercings. Neither is it necessary to play bird games and race dairy cows on game systems (although games do provide viable bonding experiences if the screen doesn't flash around like a strobe light and throw you into a seizure).

One way to connect is to learn from the young, such things as: what a browser is, smiley faces can take the place of punctuation, your new tennis shoes are skateboarding shoes, and how to get a photo right side up on a social media site. Show them you recognize and appreciate their expertise. And don't make fun of them when they ask, "Who is Roy Rogers?" or "What is Vaudeville?"

To appeal to the younger set, it helps to actively participate in their world. Even more important, is to have a passion for life and a sense of purpose. Otherwise you live in the past and tell the same old stories over and over, boring everyone into oblivion. Do you really want to be that person?

Share your wisdom. No one will know how wise and wonderful you are if you don't engage them. Avoid a preachy tone, though. Don't assume your beliefs are right for everyone. You can be gloriously opinionated if you demonstrate curiosity and respect for the opinions of others. There is something splendid about an older person opening up their mind and rethinking a long-held opinion.

Consider the power in this message: "Just by *being,* you are *enough.*" Everyone is enough just by virtue of their existence. This is a powerful message to give to young people wrestling with self-worth and to older folks struggling with relevance.

Each life is like a streaking comet to the universe. However, because each person is a part of something as magnificent as the universe, they matter. Refuse to disappear into a Garbo-esque retreat. Be a relevant participant in the realm in which you exist. Engage, show an interest in others —young, old, and in between. In spite of the overwhelming nature of the universe, you are as important as the stars, and so is everyone else.

If you accept that you are irrelevant,
you will be irrelevant.

Chapter 4

CAPTURE YOUR LIFE STORY

*Your Life is your message. . .*Gandhi

People are made of memories, but remembrances are fragile and easily lost forever. People forget, or they die, and their memories die with them. Memoir preserves the essence of a person and assures that a lifetime of wisdom is perpetuated. It supplies a platform for sharing experiences with future generations.

Imagine one of your descendants, generations from now, finding a book of your life story in an attic. They would, no doubt, look at it in awe and say, "Wow!" Envision the wonderment you would feel if you discovered a chronicle of the life of one of your ancestors. You would say, "Wow!" Someone will be touched by your story someday—if you write it.

Four-year-old Candy discovered her grandma's memoir. She carried the book around, admiring the pictures, and pretending to read it. Later, her mother salvaged it from the toy box. Although Grandma hoped Candy wouldn't read it until she was old enough to understand that Nana was not always a good role model, the book's mere existence made an impression. Someday Candy will read it, and her children, and their children, and on and on. Perhaps Candy will write a book one day because her grandma did.

In spite of the fabulous benefits of chronicling life, there are common objections to doing so, such as thinking it is self-centered to write about oneself. This conclusion undervalues a person's relevance and assumes they don't matter. If you experience an uncomfortable sense of self-aggrandizement when contemplating writing your story, remember this: *Your life is a gift. Share it.*

You might feel your history is not interesting. It is. Things that are ordinary now will be fascinating years from now when the world is different. Also, your choices and those of your ancestors brought your descendants to where they are today. This information is priceless. You never know which sweeping changes or minor details in your life will change the life of another person years from now. Incidents that initially appear to be serendipity are often explained by fascinating inter-generational influences revealed by memoir.

Life is a mosaic of moments, and future generations benefit from knowing how you, their ancestor, experienced them. Also, peers, classmates, and those in the community where you grew up will appreciate your story because it is their story, too:

> I wrote in my memoir how, as children, we celebrated May Day. On May 1st, beautifully decorated baskets filled with candy were delivered to porches. We yelled, "May basket!" and ran like crazy as kids raced out from hiding places to catch and kiss us.
>
> A neighbor I grew up with read my memoir. On the next May 1st, a UPS man delivered a May basket from her Florida home to my Oklahoma porch.
>
> This was fifty-some years since I received one. Had I realized sooner he was delivering a May basket, I would have surely chased down that UPS deliveryman and given him a May Day kiss.
>
> On may 1st the following year, UPS delivered a May basket to Florida from me.

Memoir reinforces connections. The writer of a memoir was shocked by her sudden popularity with nieces and nephews at a family reunion. After years of the younger set showing little interest in her, they jostled to sit at her picnic table. Having read her book, they had decided Aunt Shelby was way cooler than they thought. Stories of their parents and other characters fascinated them. They wanted more.

In addition to such joys, memoirs provide opportunities to impart wisdom. By documenting life experiences and lessons learned, you may at some point be the only voice of reason that influences a young person teetering on the edge of a bad decision. Through memoir, knowledge is shared whether you are still around or not. This is legacy squared.

It is tough to decide what to put in and what to leave out of a memoir. Be gentle with people and yourself, but accept that life is not always a civilized business. Don't be afraid to reveal flaws or missteps—yours or those of others. An honest life story, complete with wrong turns and regrets, demonstrates how such experiences are overcome. Being candid also helps others feel better about their own human frailties.

A memoir is not a confessional, though. You don't have to write about everything. Omissions are okay. But be brave. Almost everyone runs their life off into the ditch at some point. Lives are built on the bones of accidents, blunders, poor decisions, relations gone feral, and other misadventures. When shared, your rally from such experiences becomes an antibiotic for the foolish, youthful mistakes of others.

The reader is not the only one to benefit from a life story. The writer is rewarded as well. Capturing your story requires a *life review*, which is a cathartic, introspective activity inherent in the memoir process.

This self-reflection entails adult observations of yourself as a child. As you interpret your past with a mature perspective, gleeful good times that had been overpowered for years by bad memories are revealed. Conversely, by reflecting on the traumas, vulnerabilities are exposed that validate the fear and suffering they provoked. With this retrospection, you marvel at the grit and fortitude of the innocent child you once were. You fall in love with that child. Then, more magic. You fall in love with the adult that child became. Forgiveness beckons—for yourself and for others. Here is the result of one man's *life review*:

> Writing my story forced me to look at my past with fresh eyes. A robust sense of my history emerged. I realized how it shaped the person I am today. Amazed that I survived it all, I understood hurtful experiences and celebrated the person I became in spite of them.
>
> With the maturity of a seasoned adult, I realized people in my life did the best they could with what they had and what they knew. I forgave them for lapses and misdeeds. The weight of bitterness lifted. As I reflected on my mistakes, I forgave myself. And I forgave my children for making some of the same mistakes I made—those I so desperately tried to spare them.

If you don't have confidence in your ability to pull off a memoir, don't take the process too seriously. Create your own orbit. Write in a notebook or a journal. Write legacy poetry. Turn true stories into fiction. Write a story about something you dreamed of doing but never did. (See examples in the back of this book.) Whatever. You can write with flair and embellish with humor and outrageous tales, or you can simply state the facts. You can do the dance of emotions or keep it mellow. You can follow the rules of grammar and spelling—or not. No one is going to grade your paper. *It's not important you have a perfect story. It is just important you have one.*

You don't have to be "a writer." A quirky, flawed memoir has its own charm. You are telling your story, not producing a literary marvel. Write whatever helter-skelter, whacked-out story you want. Likewise, the medium is not important. Use a video, recorder, notebook, journal, or computer

Don't worry about looking stupid. In the movie *Smokey and the Bandit*, Burt Reynolds said to his high-toned girlfriend, who put him down because he knew nothing about ballet, "It depends on what part of the country you're standing in as to how dumb you are."

A policeman drove a friend home from a social. He remarked to his passenger as they approached an intersection, "People

will run that stop sign." His passenger
didn't take the comment seriously until in
subsequent months he noticed broken glass
and auto debris in that intersection several
times from accidents—just as the policeman,
an expert in such matters, had predicted.

You are an expert on your life. What you know
is fascinating. A wealth of stories, lush with the
potential to entertain and to convey lessons learned,
are in your head. When you preserve and share them,
your peers, the young, and future generations benefit.

Live with intention and write with purpose.
Whether intending to or not, everyone shows generations
that follow how to live, how to age, and how to die—or
perhaps how *not* to do those things. *It is impossible to
convey a neutral message.*

Most preconceived notions about aging are not
positive. Memoir is a mechanism to change that. By
capturing your stories, you not only share history and
wisdom, you demonstrate that you are still relevant.
Writing your story is a function of aging well.
Sharing it is aging *beyond* well.

———————————

*After I wrote my story, I understood for the first time,
how much my life mattered. And I realized how my
remaining years could matter.*

I may look like a sweet potato root today, but I was foxy and a lot of fun in high school. So I wrote about that. Next I wrote about an old folks' bus tour. The stories were different in content but similar in substance.

Your memoir is not supposed to be perfect. It's supposed to be finished. When my memoir was completed, I experienced an incredible sense of relief, knowing I would not die with my story still in me.

Memoir revealed the patterns (themes) in my life that explained choices. I saw myself in a fresh light. I understood the motivations behind mistakes and the paths I took. As a result, I changed for the better.

Your life matters. Now make it matter to others. . .
Roger Rosenblatt

---

1. **What form can capturing life stories take? Book? Journal? Notebook? Video?**

2. **What if you believe you can't write?**

3. **Do you believe your life is not interesting?**

4. **How do you share wisdom without being preachy?**

5. **What if there are experiences in your past you don't want to share? Are omissions a lie?**

6. **Isn't it egotistical to write about yourself? How do you avoid too much "I" in your story?**

7. **How can technology support the memoir process?**

8. **Is genealogy a better way to capture family history?**

CLOSING COMMENTS:

Through memoir, the past connects with the future, and generations link together in a common thread. This implies a responsibility to make good decisions when documenting a life story. It is a challenge to know what to share and what to leave out. What can others handle, especially the young? One lady contemplated the question of what to reveal after this experience:

> I was stocking up on sympathy cards at the grocery store when a young check-out fellow asked, "What happened?" He must have concluded there had been a catastrophe—a tornado or earthquake he hadn't heard about. Without thinking, I said, "At my age, people you know die." He didn't respond, and his face took on a concerned expression.
>
> What I said was the truth, but do young people need to know the truth?

People dying were not on that clerk's radar, at least not until I put it there. He was blissfully unaware of such prospects until my gloomy portrayal of the circumstances around sympathy cards created a negative perception.

There are better ways to convey the truth, and there are more positive truths to be shared. Perhaps I should have told the clerk I bought those cards for a craft project.

Your way of being in the world—your orienting axis—can depict strength, productivity, creativity, learning, joy, and other nurturing qualities. Or it can paint you as a fearful weakling complaining about being in the throes of a technological quagmire, living in fear of a transient ischemic attack, enduring a pacemaker that opens garage doors, coping with a savagely deteriorating dental condition, or lamenting that people you know are dying.

Through your stories and how you live, you can give others hope for a bright future. Share your stories in a way that teaches and generates hope. And remember, memoir is a forever gift.

You may believe: "I'll have time to write my story later." The truth is: Maybe. Maybe not.

Chapter 5

CONNECTIONS: FINDING A TRIBE

A garden of friends.

Humans are tribal by nature. They have a basic need to be part of a group. As you age, you may slip into the comfortable world of inactivity and isolation. Exuberance and engagement drop off the agenda. When this happens, something vital is missing—a tribe.

To be a positive role model, you must have fun. An ideal vehicle for having fun is a tribe. Connections rich with possibilities include those with friends and relatives from your youth. When reconnecting, it doesn't take long to relive memories, so orchestrating new ones is essential. Meeting in wonderful destinations, taking road trips together, or visiting in each other's homes and communities can

yield fun adventures and bonding opportunities. Here
is one such experience:

My high school girlfriends and I
realized after the loss of a classmate
around the time of our forty-year
reunion that we should stop talking
about getting together and do it. So we
took a road trip up the coast of California.
Silly high school friends again, one might
consider old gals from Iowa incapable
of terrorizing California, but we did. We
stopped at a roadside store late at night in
a quest for food where we encountered
law enforcement—a patrolman and a
sheriff's deputy in for coffee.

They were cute with their uniforms,
badges, weapons, holsters, handcuffs,
stun guns, flashlights, and radio gear.
Enchantingly festive, or so we thought,
we struck up a conversation. This
included educating them on the fact that
Iowa stands for *Idiots Out Wandering
Around*. We asked if they would like to
hear one of our high school cheers. They
agreed, somewhat hesitantly, so we lined
up and executed our favorite cheer.

By all indications, everyone in the
store was fascinated when we ended with
a maneuver reminiscent of a jump with
splits, at least as close to one as women
in their late fifties could get within the

constraints of the grocery racks, lotto machine, coin changer, and ATM.

Although the officers were in a state of shock, along with a store clerk and several patrons, we were overcome with enthusiasm and asked if they would like to hear our school song. Someone said, "No," but the officers seemed up for it, so we belted out *Beer, Beer for Old Connors High* with gusto.

This was pressing our fun because one of the officers asked if we had been drinking. I responded, "We don't got no-o-o-o-o wine coolers." To distract him, I asked, "If I lie down on the sidewalk outside, would you draw around me with that chalk you guys carry around?" Concerned the officers might interpret the lying down on the sidewalk suggestion as solicitation, my friends dragged me away.

We had so much fun that we've taken other trips since. We've never been arrested, although when I report our escapades to my daughter, she says, "Don't call me if you get thrown in jail."

Social interaction over coffee is an ideal way to create connections, especially for retired people. Find a coffee partner or two, set a routine time and place to meet, and invite others to participate. Soon you'll have a robust coffee group congregating on a regular basis. This is easy to pull off because there are coffee shops everywhere and there is a need for this type of informal interaction.

Name your group. *Pillars of Sloth* (a name that belies the productive lifestyles of its members) is a group that meets every week for coffee. A flavor of their interactions is revealed in the example of turning memoir into fiction at the end of this book.

Their focus is on fun, which means ground rules apply. No talk about politics or religion. These topics spark controversy. Our society is so polarized today by a hostile, biased media and an unfortunate political environment that strong feelings abound. Discussions around aches and pains are also avoided.

It is natural to gravitate to those who think like you. And that's okay. However, it is enlightening to socialize with people who are different. When you put judgment aside and interact with all kinds of people, your life is enriched—as long as people are not so negative that they suck the life out of you. It is okay to abandon toxic connections that bring you down.

Groups are awesome, but sometimes you just need a friend, one who is gentle and listens—one who brings you ice cream. At other times, when you say you're okay and you're not, you need a friend bold enough to tell you so. Occasionally, you need a friend who allows you to steal a bit of their shine.

Reach out. Cultivate a garden of friends. When working, a person interacts with people every day, but this often does not translate into connections outside of work. Once retired, work relationships fade, quicker than you might think. If you don't initiate opportunities to interact with people, you may find yourself without a tribe and buried in isolation.

After retirement, hunkering down and being alone initially feels comfortable. Life is peaceful and devoid of distractions. You are just mellowing out with your spouse. Over time, this solitude may not work well. The spirit craves interaction and nurturing. The solution is a tribe.

I take toxic people who suck the life out of me out of my world and seek connections with people who champion me and lift me up. They are my tribe.

A good friend can be better than a B-12 shot.

I call my crazy friends "outliers." Their uniqueness is what I love most about them.

Be inclusive. When you find yourself looking down on someone, remember this: There are no others.

Everyone is deserving of God's grace. . .Kelly Walter

My friends are diverse. One invited me to a symphony orchestra performance at The Arts Center. Another asked me to stand up with her at her wedding at The Reformed Criminals Biker Rally.

When my girlfriends talk about trips to the Greek Islands, Dubai, Paris, Rome, or London, I tell them about my trip to Muskogee, Oklahoma.

In spite of occasions to mix with the socially elite, I have no interest in making a connection there. (I have never worn jewelry to a swimming pool.) On the occasions when I wandered into this community, I thought, "I gave up cowboys for this?"

My friend was choking on something at dinner. I patted her on the back. A guy friend patted her on the chest. Which technique worked is unknown, but I rewarded the fellow by brushing crumbs onto his lap and then brushing them off. We all look out for each other.

---

1. **How vital are connections? Are there people who don't need them?**

2. **How do you go about finding a tribe? Can you create one of your own?**

3. **Should you strive for diversity or commonality in your connections? Why?**

4. **How do you manage conflict if your group is made up of diverse members?**

5. **How can you deal with an increasingly polarized society that complicates relationships?**

6. **What advantages do mixed-gender groups have?**

7. **Can technology enhance connectedness?**

8. **Can service opportunities lead to connections?**

9. **Can you have too many connections?**

10. **How do relationships change as you move through the decades of aging?**

_____

CLOSING COMMENTS:

There are several avenues for forming your own tribe. One is to host regular get-togethers for people with common interests. A standard meeting time and place is helpful. Familiarity is appealing. The place becomes a "clubhouse" of sorts. It can be your home, a cafe, coffeeshop, community center, or any public place. Food is a major attraction. Rotating food preparation allows participants to show off recipes and everyone doesn't have to prepare something for every meeting.

To add structure and to encourage interaction, devote a portion of each meeting to a presenter or announce a pre-determined topic for group discussion. When participants *are* the program, sharing bonds them together as long as controversial topics are avoided.

For a book club, it is not necessary that everyone read the same book. Attendees can talk about whatever they are reading. Encourage them to share books and to read excerpts from their favorites. When people *are* the program, the wonder unfolds.

Community centers are worth checking out. They offer games and activities that facilitate making connections. Meals and all manner of offerings may be available.

Devoting yourself to serving others is also a lucrative and productive avenue for connecting. There are no shortages of needy organizations looking for helpers. You may find a tribe there. You may also find passion, purpose, and bliss.

A sense of belonging through relationships with others is vital to aging *beyond* well. If you can't find a tribe that is a good fit, form one of your own. Evolve. Reach out. Find your tribe(s).

One goal of a tribe should be to have fun.
Always have fun. You can never have too much fun.

Chapter 6

LOVE: A FINE, FANCIFUL FRENZY—OR NOT

I don't understand the opposite sex any better at sixty than I did at sixteen.

A five-year-old asked his father, "When I get married do I get to pick a wife or do I have to take what I get and not throw a fit?" Dad was perplexed by the question until Mom explained, "When a kid complains at preschool that someone else got more Kool-Aid than he did, he is told, 'Take what you get and don't throw a fit.'"

People often settle for what they can get because finding enduring love is a long shot—one similar to locating a missing sock in the dryer. It's like "a dating Siberia" out there, so they surrender to a love interest that is everything they want and nothing they need. To avoid a harrowing experience, men should be wary of women bearing casseroles. Women should ask themselves, "Do I really want to be the one who won the casserole war?" To some, love is like falling into a vat of caramel—sweet, messy, and deliciously sticky—but it can also be annoying.

Too often I stand in the kitchen peeling potatoes and smashing garlic cloves while my man mellows out on the sofa with the remote. This causes me to wonder what happened to the Bonnie Raitt music I used to play while preparing a bowl of cereal for my supper when I was single.

His bird dog has taken over my spot on the sofa. If my man had to choose, I would most likely lose out to his drooling, panting canine. Then he washes my car, vacuums the interior, checks the spare, fills up the gas tank, and I decide to keep him.

Our home is his environment. I cannot listen to Aretha Franklin while dusting. Instead, TV blares with Bonanza, NASCAR, Die Hard, a UFO conspiracy film, a Loch Ness monster feature, or a Big Foot scientific documentary. And he makes fun of me when I watch the *Home and Garden Channel*. Then he nurses me through a health crisis, and I decide to keep him.

When TV is not on, the stereo is. If I hear *Free Bird* one more time on surround sound, I'll go insane. His lack of awareness makes me wonder if he had mold in his sippy cup as a toddler. I'd be better served by a man who thinks he is interesting because he collects salt and pepper shakers. Then my man does the dishes. No doubt he would rather reupholster a recliner than do dishes. So, although he doesn't wipe off the counters, I decide to keep him.

To make rational love choices—if such a thing is possible—it helps to understand this: *What matters most in a relationship is how each person makes the other one feel.* Nothing else matters as much as that. If love makes you feel good, you've got it going on. Keep in mind, though, that wine also does that, and so does chocolate.

Love is seductive. Regardless of protestations, the search is on. Many seek a partner through the Internet. This can be described as drive-by-dating. A man eliminated a prospect pictured in her online profile on a plaid Herculon upholstered sofa holding a picture of Elvis. A woman said of her experience, "The date reminded me of changing my mind about having a baby while in the delivery room." She also complained that overweight, balding men were looking for women who were athletic, fit, and toned.

People who lie on the Internet complain that people lie on the Internet. A woman who lied about her age and weight griped, "He lied. He's not 5'11, and he smokes." Many lie by omission.

A woman picked a fellow up at the airport whom she met on a dating site. Both his eye teeth were missing. (He wasn't smiling in his online photos.) She brought him to dinner with friends. Missing the self-awareness gene, the fellow smiled frequently and broadly.

Her shocked friends laughed a bit too heartily when anyone said something funny. And when they laughed he laughed, and then they laughed some more, and then he laughed, and then . . .well, you get the picture.

Though popular, online dating is not the answer for everyone. Going out to bars is not the answer either. You risk meeting someone who goes to the liquor store for breakfast and asks you to blow into a breathalyzer so they can drive. You also risk drinking too much and asking, "Am I sexy yet?"

I went out one night with friends who followed a band around town. We were out of our element in an unfortunate club that resembled a prison visiting room. There, a man with missing teeth, clearly on his own unicorn, approached me and said, "You are prettier than a can of pork and beans." With a single upper front tooth, my admirer reminded me of a can opener. If I were to go camping, he might come in handy. But I don't go camping. Not comprehending *no* as a complete sentence, he clung to me like a tree frog. A guy friend rescued me by asking him, "What part of *no* do you not understand?"

One lady had this advice on dating. "Get up early for breakfast dates to avoid sheet marks on your face. If a man requests a casserole, direct him to the casserole fairy. And, when you see young people humping each other on a dance floor, tell your date up front, 'We won't be doing that.'"

Children frequently have issues with their older parents' love connections, and for good reason. A partner can be a financial and emotional threat. Other relatives and friends can also throw a kink into a relationship. Then there is the reality that one partner is going to die before the other—another loss to endure. With these prospects facing her, one lady concluded, "I don't have another breakup in me." A man said, "I'd rather be an oil soaked bird."

Both men and women occasionally swear off love completely. They say, "Never," and mean it. But love is a tempting mistress. A bitter man who had sworn off love saw a foxy woman and the chase was on. Someone asked a lady in her seventies facing a serious medical condition if there was anything she wanted to do while she was still able. She said, "Dear God, just give me one more boyfriend."

Others determinedly deny love's potential. One man stated his position, "When it comes to love, I'd rather be in the vortex of a tornado, assemble an Ikea bookcase, or convert my computer operating system to OS-X-Snowbird 1200-6.20, or. . ." A woman in a similar state of mind admitted:

> Syrupy thoughts still occasionally creep into my mind, but I'm afraid we will be dancing at a wedding and he will drop to the floor and do the gator. Or he will tell my girlfriends that a man jacks up his truck because fat girls can't climb. Or he'll grow a beard and turn into a Chia Pet. So I romanticize about the unattainable—pirates, robots, and Gene Hackman. The problem with this is, if I come across a robot, I will no doubt say to him "Oh, there you are. I've been looking for you all my life."

An inevitable dance of emotions is tied to love. The passion it generates introduces an absence of rational thought. People are on it like a rat on cheese. A woman who had sworn off love is swept away by a man with a rakish swagger. A man runs across a woman as cute as a spotted pup and is determined to adopt her. The need is palpable, the temptations real. But perhaps too much value is attributed to romantic love. Perhaps friendship is a better bet.

The ghost of an unfortunate lost love may have left tattoos on the heart that thwart potential relationships. Rumi said, "The wound is the place that lets the light in." This suggests that love is almost always achievable if sought in earnest.

———————————

*You know that look women get when they want to have sex? Me neither. . .*Steve Martin

*There is some dance in the old dame yet. . .*Mahitabel

I relate to a man the same way I would to a lost puppy. I'd take him home, feed him, and play with him until he found his forever home.

Men are a lot of trouble. I got pregnant once while trying to help my husband quit smoking.

I've moved out of the pet me and I'll purr stage, and it no longer does any good for a man to throw chocolate at me. A Jaguar—maybe.

I thought the old gals were going to "cane bang" me for not bringing food to a potluck dinner. I got away with that all my life. What has changed?

We compromise nicely on things. She wants to watch a chick flick. I want to watch an action movie. We compromise and watch a chick flick.

Love left me hard enough to roller skate on. I'm cynical. My love objective now is to fail better.

He winked at me several times. I assumed he was flirting, so I winked back. Turns out he had a tic.

I chatted online with a man who turned out to be so Irish I knew if he hung around very long I would want him to go be Irish someplace else.

Avoid anyone who, when you are going out to dinner, asks, "What are you all dressed up for?"

She was a mess when I picked her up for a date. I advised, "It's not a good idea to drink and dress."

A homing device in my uterus allows me to locate misplaced keys, remotes, and shotgun shells. Who died and left me in charge of ammunition?

I once thought a man was mysterious because he was quiet only to discover later he was just stupid.

I've never felt like I needed to change. I've always thought if you want someone different, pick someone else. . .Melissa McCarthy

You teach people how to treat you. . .Dr. Phil

I can't find a man because I'm overqualified.

My friend saw a man and said, "I'd climb that tree."

Some issues are between you and yourself. When people show you who they really are, and you don't believe them, it's your fault, not theirs.

———————————

1. **Is there a point where love is no longer desired?**

2. **How important is love to aging *beyond* well?**

3. **What are the unique complications of late-in-life love? How are children affected?**

4. **How viable is online dating as a way to connect?**

5. **How do reasons to be married (or not) change when people are older?**

6. **Can a non-romantic connection be enough?**

———————————

CLOSING COMMENTS:

A little sister said to her older brother, "It's okay if you don't tell me you love me." He responded, "I do love you. I just don't know it." That says a lot about the differences between the sexes.

> Older people sometimes act like children. A guy left his tools in the living room, so his woman put makeup in his tool box. In her mind, her action was a defensible, mature response. She said, "Well, he started it."

With so many complexities and hurdles, life on the periphery of love may be worth exploring. Friendships are less contrived and often as richly nurturing as romantic love. Consider residing in the crevices of love by focusing on friendships. It is possible to harness the synergy of multiple friendships through coed packs. These associations allow for the enjoyment of connections with groups of people without obligations or complications.

Finding love late in life is similar to searching for a palm tree in Detroit. And it can sting. Nevertheless, it is an opiate. You can pretend it doesn't matter, but it does. It matters a lot. The redeeming factor is that love comes in many forms. Romantic love is not for everyone. You can seek the splendor of that—or not.

> *Before engaging, ask yourself, "Does this person make me better?" If not, move on.*

Chapter 7

SIMPLIFY EVERYTHING

It's just stuff.

Clutter buries the spirit and haunts those you love. If you have macramé in your closet, at some point it is likely to traumatize them. They may hurt themselves laughing.

Possessions are problematic. They require storage, maintenance, and sometimes defense.

A gated community with a lovely pool was invaded frequently by a teenage girl, with attitude, from a nearby neighborhood. She climbed the fence to access the pool, bringing friends along. The teens generally left the area in a mess. When confronted, the entitlement-minded girl argued, "Basically, like the pool is here, and like you aren't basically like using it." Homeowners explained that pool insurance provisions prohibited use by unauthorized non-residents. The girl and her friends kept coming.

So a couple of men went to the girl's home with a cooler, a six pack, and a sack of groceries, rang the doorbell and informed the parents that, since no one was like using their patio, basically they and their friends were like going to like borrow it for a barbecue. They would probably like get drunk, smoke cigars, and basically leave any residue.

The parents, unaware of their daughter's pool invasions, got the message, and like they responded appropriately. The men were good neighbors and like left the groceries, and like that was the end of that, basically.

Residents have to deal with the ramifications of having a pool. Possessions generate consequences. When you have nice things, others want to enjoy them. Also, the more possessions you have, the less money you have. People rarely evaluate whether possessions are worth the cost and trouble they interject. They fail to consider alternative uses of money, space, and time.

Once procured, belongings are often hoarded long after their usefulness has faded. This attachment to material possessions results in an accumulation that complicates the aging process. George Carlin performed a comedy routine about people and their stuff—how they acquire it, maintain it, insure it, shuffle it around, lose it, find it, pay to store it, take it on vacation, loan it out, try to get it back, worry about it, protect it, and move cars out of garages into driveways to accommodate it.

Consumer excesses and a pack-rat mentality drive people to fill houses, attics, sheds, yards, storage units, and parents' and friends' homes. To reframe aging, you must go lean and mean.

> An elderly lady went into a nursing home with just enough stuff to fill a dresser. Her daughters worried about emptying out her house, but she said, "Do with my things what you will. It's just stuff."

This is unusual. Most people find it difficult to give up possessions. It is especially hard to get rid of heirlooms or items that were gifts. But it *is* just stuff. Most likely, those who gave you things didn't intend for you to keep them forever. There may be people who would value those items if you can bring yourself to give them away. Here is my approach to keeping my environment simple:

> Once a year I go through every cupboard, drawer, crook and cranny of my house, garage, and attic and get rid of

things. I make three piles: *keep, toss,* and *give away.* My criteria for discarding something is: Will my daughter think I'm gonzo when she discovers it after I'm gone? Will it create a dilemma for her to have to decide what to do with it? Can I convert it to cash or can someone else enjoy it?

I don't keep things because I might need them later. I ask myself this: *If I need it later, can I procure another one?* If doing so is not expensive, I get rid of the item. I keep only one of everything—one set of tools, one set of dishes, and one set of silverware. My daughter admires my home when she visits.

In the last trimester of life, you don't need much. Each decade you need less. At some point, you don't even need a car or a house.

A man disposed of his father's assets, distributed the sentimental items among family members, and settled his dad into a nursing home. His father's possessions had been reduced to what would fit into a dresser and a file box full of papers.

When his father died, the items in the nursing home were similarly disposed of. What remained was the box. His father's life had come down to a box.

Eventually, everyone's life comes down to a box. This is the cycle of life. Possessions are on loan.

For most people, the most tedious problem with stuff springs from little things, a lifetime accumulation of trinkets, souvenirs, heirlooms, antiques, gadgets, clothes, and all manner of paper products. The task of sorting through such a stash is enormous. At some point, it must be done. If you don't take on the project, you will leave a colossal mess for loved ones. They are reminded of that burden every time they see your stuff, which creates dread. Do you want to do that to them?

Post-retirement is an ideal time to reevaluate stuff, to organize it, or remove it from your world and theirs. Thoreau said, "We are happy in proportion to the things we can do without." Einstein also had advice on stuff, "Out of clutter find simplicity."

Books are hard to part with. You believe you will read them again, but you don't. Instead, you accumulate more, as this lady did:

> I experienced a long-running period of reading crime books. I call that my *Fathoming the Sociopath Period.* I have shelves of these books. While checking out at a book store one day, the cashier noted several books about women killing their husbands. *Black Widow* was splashed across the covers.
>
> My husband stood behind me with a book on wiring for surround sound. The clerk asked him if my book selections

made him nervous. He responded, "It
hadn't, but it does now." In my mind, his
book was the real threat. Surround sound
and The Grateful Dead had the potential
to ruin my life.

Most likely, no one will fight over the crime
books when this woman is gone, but more valuable
items can create fractures among loved ones. You can
proactively discourage this outcome by being
generous with assets while you are still able and by
planning for the distribution of your estate.

In addition to paring down possessions,
shedding habits and beliefs that no longer serve you
well simplifies life. Obligations, such as cooking for
holidays or storing children's stuff in your home are
candidates for abandonment.

Volunteering can be limited to only those
activities you are most passionate about. If you limit
commitments to those appropriate for this time in
your life, you will let a lot of obligations go. Doing
so frees up time and money.

It is important to simplify financial matters as
well. Legal fees required to deal with a mess of assets
and investments can eat away at an estate.

I have one checking account, one
savings account, one IRA, and one each
of health, life, and long-term care
insurance. I have one house and one car,

both insured. When I received stock valued at $600 in a legal settlement, I immediately sold it. The value of it could have easily been eaten up by legal fees if it ended up in my estate. I gave many of my assets and heirlooms away. I kept the dog. He keeps squirrels from eating the patio furniture, and his presence forces me to vacuum the house every six months whether it needs it or not.

Simplifying everything and moving out of the acquisition mode reduces consumption. A surprising amount of money and time is reclaimed. Assets are put to better use. (Gifting them to others is a gift to yourself.) Also, living simply introduces space in which to create.

Possessions are links in chains around your neck. . .Thoreau

Simplicity is the greatest sign of sophistication. . .da Vinci

"Your home should rise up to greet you when you enter.". . .Oprah Winfrey

Un-clutter your surroundings and you will un-clutter your mind.

I have simplified my life by cutting living costs. I use half as much shampoo, dish detergent, laundry products, etc. I have eliminated paper products. I freeze leftovers and pay attention to utility costs. I have stopped paying people to do things for me. I wash my car, clean my house, color my hair, and polish my nails. I go to the library instead of buying magazines and books. I drink free water in restaurants. The savings are incredible, and I actually enjoy the austerity. I feel less wasteful and more responsible.

I take a certain amount of cash out of the bank and try to make it last as long as possible. I'm amazed at how long I can go without going back to the well. The frugality frees me from the clutches of consumerism.

I reduced my footprint on the planet. I was bi-sactual. —using both paper and plastic sacks. With reusable bags, I'm now tri-sactual because I still use paper or plastic when I forget to take reusable bags to the store.

I'm no longer a good capitalist. When I drive by a store and am tempted to go in, I think about something else I can do that is a better use of my time—something fun that doesn't complicate my life with an acquisition.

All my life I wrestled with time. Once retired, time became gentle. It is now my friend. And time introduces space in which to come to terms with my stuff.

When the money was rolling in, I ignored it rolling out. Contemplating those wasteful years, I regret them. I'm so over those spending and acquiring impulses.

---

1. **How do society and marketing drive the compulsion to acquire and keep things?**

2. **How can you cope with getting rid of clutter?**

3. **What do you do with things you're eliminating?**

4. **What criteria can you use to decide what to get rid of? How do you handle sentimental items?**

5. **How do you know what is valuable to others, so you don't give away items someone else values?**

6. **How do you divvy up possessions in a way that people don't fight over them?**

7. **How can you go about simplifying your life from a financial perspective?**

8. **How do you simplify your commitments?**

9. **In what other ways can you simplify your life?**

———————————

CLOSING COMMENTS:

Many times when something is acquired, it creates a problem. Where to put it? How to fit it in? How to maintain it? When you are no longer an obsessed consumer, such problems are avoided. By abandoning the role of a gullible muse to the marketplace and by developing a symbiotic relationship with simplicity, you no longer hear malls calling your name. You don't think, "What can I buy?" You think, "What can I do?" *You move from acquiring to experiencing.*

This can significantly enrich your life. Consider applying this criteria when the temptation to acquire lurks: When something is bought, something else must go. To reevaluate spending, you might experiment with your tolerance for frugality:

> I did a two-month test to determine if I could live on Social Security. There were hard sacrifices, but I did it. Once I realized this scenario wasn't a major catastrophe, I was no longer a hostage to fear. I knew I could survive. New habits were formed that I continued to apply after the trial was over. I became a better citizen of the planet. That felt good.

By not managing your stuff, you set the stage for your worst nightmare: those you care about fighting over your possessions when you are gone. The solution: be generous. Once you have enough money to be secure, why not give the rest away? Divvy up possessions while you are still here so you can referee the process and watch others enjoy the treasures. When someone admires a possession, give it to them, keeping in mind fairness to others and any previous commitments. Use money to create family bonding experiences, such as family reunions, vacations, and celebrations. Be a sponsor.

Getting rid of clutter is freeing, but it is a baffling and uncomfortable process for people who have spent their lives accumulating.

> While moving into senior housing, a lady's children persuaded her to let go of a number of shabby possessions. Doing so was a challenge, but she ended up bringing only a few items with her. The kids bought her new furniture, linens, decorations, and kitchen items. This fresh start was something she'd never experienced. The change mystified her at first, but she soon acclimated. In fact, she became a tad uppity. She said, "Those other old folks' places are junked up."

Imagine those you care about going through your possessions when you are gone or when you must downsize into more appropriate housing. They will probably enjoy sifting through some of the memorabilia, photos, journals, and personal items. However, if you've kept so much stuff that your place resembles the debris field of an airplane crash, they will say, "Look at all this junk. What a mess." If you've managed your stuff well, they are likely to say, "Wow. Dad has nice things. Let's divide them up."

A will can describe a fun and fair way to distribute possessions, one that discourages conflict.

> Beneficiaries gather at the home of the deceased, draw numbers, and take turns selecting items. Then the selection process is reversed. The person who chooses last on the first round chooses first on the second, and so on. This process can be fun if clutter is discarded and only worthy items remain.

Send a clear message that you care enough about others to manage possessions in a way that doesn't burden them when you are gone or when you must move. Reevaluate belongings so when people visit they don't look around and dread the day they have to deal with a mess. Go drawer by drawer, closet by closet, and room by room and simplify.

Don't haunt people you care about with your stuff. Keep it lean and mean. Be generous with the finer things. Give them away. The true legacy of your life will be determined by how you lived and what you gave to others, not what you held on to until the end.

The most important element of simplifying life has little to do with you and everything to do with those you care about.

Chapter 8

HEALTH AND FITNESS

*I wish I weighed what I weighed
when I first thought I was fat.*

Is the aging fairy sucker punching you? Are body parts moving around, downward mostly? Do you resemble Jabba the Hutt? Do people beep when you back up? Are you and your dance partner bumping bellies? Do your arms resemble swim floaties? Does back fat make it appear as though a bulletproof vest is nestled under your shirt? Does your body function as if it were bought at Ikea and whoever put it together didn't follow the instructions?

Do you brag about glucose levels rather than career accomplishments and exotic travel experiences? Are you taking enough drugs to open your own pharmacy? Are sexual exploits limited to near sex experiences?

If so, and you decide to do something about it, beware. You may become so fit that you find yourself years from now dying of nothing. Or you end up in a fitness protection program. Or young employees at fitness centers, who don't understand the nuances of the older body, hurt you.

> I joined a training facility. It was there that my personal trainer, Levi, tried to kill me. I begged for mercy, "Don't hurt me, master. Please don't hurt me." My pleas were futile.
>
> He handed me weights over twenty pounds each, and I dropped to the floor. Doing lunges while holding weights in each hand, I begged people in the training room, "Help me. Please, help me." No one responded. They had their own "Oh, my god!" scenarios going on.
>
> Levi was not letting up, and it was clearly a matter of saving myself. So I threw up.

Fitness gurus also deprive you of necessities, such as adult beverages, chicken fried bacon, and cinnamon rolls the size of your head. They don't realize that comfort food is one of the few pleasures left for older folks.

Seeking a personal trainer was an act of sheer desperation for me. I had rationalized that working out intruded too much into couch time where I ate potato chips and Oreos. For exercise I sat. As a result, I gained weight, and this happened:

My man was helping me squeeze my Size 12 body into a bustier-type bra designed for a strapless Size 8 evening gown. This bustier had the attributes of knight's armor and came down to a v-shape in the stomach area.

He hooked it in the back. I turned around to discover him staring with shock and awe at a massive and strangely out of place v-shaped roll of fat on my belly pooching out below the bustier. When he rallied enough to speak he said, "That's gonna show."

Desperate, I located a panty girdle and slipped it on over the bustier effectively eliminating the belly roll. However, this caused a significant roll of fat to materialize at the top of my thigh.

It was obvious that was going to show. So, in a panic, I traded it for a long-line girdle which produced a disturbing monumental roll of fat above the knees.

At this point my husband insisted I stop the madness. "If you go any further, you'll have fat ankles," he said, "and there ain't no way to cover that up."

Physical exercise is not the only solution to body issues. Reducing stress also helps. Coping mechanisms are useful when dealing with degrading bodily changes. One tactic is to shift your thinking like the lady who said, "I'm not fat. I'm fluffy." Okay, okay, that might not do it for you. How about my approach?

> Two words help me cope: *oh well*. I say them to myself out loud when I notice a body issue. Potent medicine is dispensed through an enthusiastic, well-timed *oh well*. This doesn't give me game, but it promotes acceptance, and that gives me game—sort of.

Another way to cope with degrading body changes is to interpret them as *patina*. Copper takes on a green tone called *patina* as it weathers. Many consider it beautiful. Imperfections on furniture, accessories, and a building can also be interpreted as *patina*. Blemishes add character. They are evidence of history—proof that the object has endured and is valued, used, and beautifully flawed. Cosmetic flaws on the body can be construed this way as well. *Patina* is achievable while perfection is a hopeless objective that sucks the life out of a person. A new version of beauty is embraced when the concept of *patina* is applied to the body.

It would be misguided, though, to suggest that all visible signs of aging are beautiful. They are not. But they are organic and pure, and they are part of still being here. *Oh well.*

———————————————

When did I go from looking good to looking good for my age?

I'm like a tire with no tread.

If I live long enough, I will become cute again.

Fitness delays the early onset of a preference for Velcro, elastic waistbands, and arch supports.

Maternity clothes from Target disguise belly fat but induce embarrassing pat downs at airport security.

The problem with fitness is that it requires exercise, which gets the heart all churned up.

If someone falls down and they get into a knee-chest position to get up—which bump and grind enthusiasts call "the spanking position"—don't spank them. Such actions have a way of coming back to bite you.

To rally from a squat position (assumed when determining how low you can go while dancing to "Shout"), try an old stripper move. Send your butt up first, and the rest will follow.

Don't be that old person looking back at his life and thinking, "If I had known I was going to live this long, I would have taken better care of myself."

I forgive myself for lapses in my health routine and start back up again. Off and on is better than nothing.

The road to hell is paved with ice cream—and cheese.

My body is so out of shape that friends must search for ways to compliment me. They tell me I have nice bone structure or fabulous eyebrows.

My body is still a wonderland. I wonder where certain parts went as they shifted around, and I wonder if and when they will stop working altogether.

I have a body that is never summer ready.

My friends and I work out for an hour three times a week. The problem is that afterward we go to Rib Crib.

As my body deteriorates, I respond by covering up body parts. I will be in a burka soon.

I tried to go vegetarian, but meat has so many vital nutritional features, such as saturated fat, estrogen, growth hormones, and antibiotics.

---

1. **How does your fitness influence others?**

2. **What if you are fit and your partner or friends are not, or vice versa?**

3. **How big a role does good balance play in fitness?**

4. **What can you do when you have to give up your favorite fitness activities?**

5. **How important is fitness to frame of mind?**

6. **If fitness extends life, is it adding good years or extending the final rough ones?**

7. **Are you mentally prepared for when physical activity is restricted?**

8. **How do you cope with physical decline? Do the concepts of *oh well* or *patina* help?**

CLOSING COMMENTS:

Whatever you do, at least do something to stay fit. If you stop working out altogether, a litany of unfortunate consequences are inevitable. One of those is poor posture. Keeping the core strong is key. Never underestimate the power of posture.

My posture has deteriorated, which stresses me out. I worry my frame will end up so stooped that someday when I'm in a wheelchair, caretakers will have to strap me in to keep me from somersaulting out. I fear becoming a person who, when seen from behind, appears to not have a head.

Don't be that person. And beware of shortcuts. They can be tricky, as this woman discovered:

Body shapers came into fashion. In a desperate attempt to rein in fat, I acquired one with panels to trim tummy and back fat. It also had sleeves designed to slim the upper arms. A marvel it was.

It was a hot day the first time I wore it. I sweated so much that every inch of that spandex straitjacket stuck to me like skin on a seal. I tried everything to get it off, but once that wonder garment bunched up around my shoulders with the sleeves still tightly stuck to my upper arms, it wasn't going anywhere. It was like being attacked by a tire tube.

Trapped in mounds of elastic stretched tightly across my shoulders, chest, and arms, I began to feel claustrophobic. The more I wrestled, twisted, and pulled the tighter it felt. Panic set in. What to do? Fat pooched out everywhere. The sight would have frightened any self-respecting fireman, so 911 was not an option. No one deserves to see that.

Finally, in an act of desperation, I located scissors and hacked my way out of that shapewear marvel. When it snapped off, body parts burst out of the elastic mass like a dog who discovered someone had left the gate open.

I was suddenly several sizes larger with flappy upper arms, a Rubenesque belly, and back fat resembling cats in a burlap sack. Cutting up that pricey elastic wonder was a costly solution, but it was a matter of saving myself.

Although an older body is an easy target for jokes, fitness is a serious subject with significant consequences. Your health matters to you and to those who care about you.

To fight the good fight, some older people engage in line dancing. Many senior centers offer such programs. There you can rumba, samba, cha-cha, Charleston, salsa, two-step, and do the Hokey Pokey—all without a partner. This is important because women outnumber men ten to one in such settings. This is fun stuff, so much so that you may decide that the Hokey Pokey *is* what it's all about.

Swimming is a good option if you can find a long-line swimsuit with sleeves. That comment comes from the "oh, cover that up" philosophy of interpreting the aging body. An alternate perspective adopted by older folks in Florida is to reveal the body with abandon. One Florida woman said, "I didn't read an article on how to get a bikini body. I know how to do that. Put on a bikini."

If you are a woman, you can go to a women's only workout center. There you do circuit training with your sisters while listening to music by Cher and contemplating the world situation; back fat; no-sugar, almond, oatmeal, raisin, flaxseed, gluten-free cookie recipes; and men who are sent to the store and return with Spiderman napkins for Thanksgiving dinner.

Yoga is good, but certain positions can make a person wonky. You may list to the non-dominant side, unless you are a man. In that case, listing is determined by the direction of the comb-over. There's no scientific data to support this premise, but it discourages comb-overs. (To avoid gender bias, it is appropriate to reflect on women's blue-hair, which is discouraged by asking if it glows in the dark.)

To go *beyond* aging well, you must engage in the fitness fight. When the reality of limitations is undeniable, focus on things you *can* do. If music and eating are on it, you're good.

It's not necessary to lose weight. All you need is software. It's virtual plastic surgery.

Chapter 9

TECHNOLOGY: KICKING AND SCREAMING INTO THE DIGITAL AGE

I will embrace the world of technology, and
I will take whatever medication is required to do so.

Technology is key to participating in the world today. It has become a primary channel for communication. To connect with children, grandchildren, and friends, you need to be at least a tad Internet savvy. If you want to see photos of them, you must get online, unless they thoughtfully give you photos. Good luck with that.

As your physical limitations gain momentum, the Internet serves as a way to connect. It is also a source for learning, a mechanism to realize dreams, and a path to relevance. Technology can be annoying, though, as this woman's experience demonstrates:

My computer gave me so much trouble that I was broke from shelling out money for geek support. Technology had defeated me. It stole my retirement dream of writing and sent me into depression—and ultimately into therapy.

My therapist suggested I get an *Apple* computer and the requisite related equipment. "It's friendly," she said, "and *Apple* offers both training and phone assistance." She promised that even a technological idiot (my term, not hers) like myself could do amazing things with an *Apple* laptop. Turns out she was right, but it has not been an easy road.

Apple services are provided primarily by delightful young geniuses, whom I call "the children." I asked "the child" who sold me the equipment, "Who can set this up for me?" He assured me, "You can do it." The prospect of my doing so was slim to none.

I was emotionally fragile at the time. Failure meant I would assume the fetal position and have fuzzy dreams about unicorns doing the Paso Doble on my bedroom ceiling. So the boxes containing computer equipment sat in my kitchen for weeks, taunting me.

Finally, one day I ate all the bacon I wanted and mustered enough courage to by golly install a computer. Determined,

I introduced a concept foreign to me—patience—and set about the task. In four hours with nine help desk calls, I installed the computer and all related devices. And I did so without crying.

At one point the help desk "child" asked me if my cookies were activated. I responded, "Well, aren't you the little rascal." When I realized there were missing cords, I called him to report that problem. After a pregnant pause, he responded, in an exceptionally slow and precise manner, "Ma'am, it is wireless." I said, "Okay. Thank you."

I contemplated the mass of wires tucked behind the computer/printer/time capsule/modem/surge protector setup. It looked like a telephone company switching station back there.

A dot at the top of the computer screen was a camera. I didn't know this, so it was a shock during the installation process to suddenly see myself pop up on that screen in faded flannel pajamas, no makeup except mascara under my eyes, and hair resembling a cat toy. The angle was not good. It showed my neck, for God's sake, and made my nose look huge and my chin recessed. It was as though I was seeing myself reflected in a spoon.

The lighting was horrible. Worst of all, there was cleavage, which generated severe panic, the kind that sets off the fight or flight response. There I was on the world-wide web looking like a slovenly trollop. Undiscriminating men all over the world would be wanting me.

Panic stricken, I rushed to my vanity for an overhaul so as to appeal to the more discriminating males. Regrouping, I adjusted the screen for a better angle, softened the lighting, and reported the problem to a help desk child who assured me no one saw it but me.

"But I'm all fixed up now," I said.

I now have tape over that dot. I don't trust it. With the computer in the kitchen, someone might see me loading the dishwasher naked.

I began writing my memoirs that afternoon. I even Googled myself. Just like Steve Martin in *The Jerk* when he discovered his name in a phone book and began yelling, "I am somebody," Google made me feel like I was somebody. This was a good thing, until it revealed that I often drive a car like I stole it.

Considerable support is typically required to introduce older people to electronics. One son said, "The worst thing I ever did was get Dad a computer." Making too many demands on children can drive them away. A lady, who had a "to do" list for her son every time he visited, soon found him showing up less often. Children like to rescue parents, but too many demands can result in them pulling back.

There are community resources available for seniors to learn how to use a computer. Spare your children the responsibility of assuring your technical literacy, unless they clearly love doing such a thing.

Technical expertise introduces a litany of opportunities The memoir process is enhanced. Stories are efficiently shared online. Electronic files are sent to printers. Photos are scanned into online albums, incorporated in memoirs, and shared on social media sites. Robust genealogy information is available through the Internet, and applications will organize and publish the results of such research.

Learning opportunities are abundant online. Connecting with old friends is facilitated. Numerous avenues for shopping and price comparisons are offered. Communication with groups of people is efficiently accomplished with just a couple of clicks. News, weather, and pollen count information is available twenty-four seven. The possibilities are endless, and most of these resources are free.

There are negatives, though. The mass of information available can be overwhelming. Some call it *Internet noise.* Unsolicited intrusions and marketing ploys are launched at you at such a rate that they rise to the nuisance level of fruit flies. There are also scammers. Older people are the target audience for bombarding marketeers, lurking viruses, and scheming manipulators. It is important you become savvy enough to avoid this invasion.

Unfortunately, a large percentage of online information is not evidence based. Designed by those determined to sway people to act against their own best interests, it is brilliantly framed but distorted, if not outright wrong. Unless you aspire to become a victim, fact-checking online information is a must.

If you are willing to go kicking and screaming into the world of technology, you can use it to reframe your aging experience. If not, don't let anyone make you feel like a dinosaur. You're not.

No matter how frustrating technology might be—and it is immensely frustrating—the benefits make it worthwhile for most older people. Opportunities to enrich their lives and the lives of those around them are significant. Email is a good place to start because it is simple and offers avenues to connect with others. Technological expertise will become more vital as you age and activities and mobility are restricted. A computer or a phone can be your window to the world.

Everything has become so complicated. Operating a remote is like flying a spaceship.

My living room television suddenly went to black and white. I had to run to the bedroom television to see what color the walls were painted on The Home and Garden Channel.

When I lost my hearing, my computer became my window to the world.

I accidentally took a picture of my feet with my phone. A child helped me post it on Facebook with the message: "I got a new phone with a camera."

I asked my grandkids, "Where should we go Saturday to stare at our phones?"

Technology and I are mutually abusive. My printer got unhappy so I told it to get out.

Friends said I needed to update my phone greeting because the background sounded like bar noise. I must have butt recorded it at Fishbones Pool Hall.

When I received email advertisements for male enhancement items while working, I forwarded them to the company security officer with the comment, "You might be interested in this." After retirement, I forwarded them to ex-boyfriends.

When WiFi has a higher ranking than makeup on your hierarchy of needs, you have crossed over.

A phone company customer service device said, "Goodbye," and hung up on me. It's irritating to be blown off with cheerful enthusiasm by a machine. So I drove to the phone store where I took a number so I could wait to be abused in person.

I didn't know how to cancel printing. It's not good to expect one page and get forty. You can run out of ink, which opens up a whole new can of worms.

I asked an electronics store clerk for a cute contraption on which to play my favorite songs. When he asked if I needed a woofer or a tweeter, I told him my landlord doesn't allow pets.

It seemed as though people disappear into the Internet, never to be seen or heard from again.

I don't have a good relationship with my GPS, so I have the car dealership set it for trips so as not to head out for Kansas City and end up in Waco.

I've been known to call Apple help desk people and say, "I'm in a bad mood, and you are going to pay." With youthful determination, they carry me away to technology nirvana.

My friend calls selfies "facies." I call them "knobbies" because they make people look as if their faces are reflected in a doorknob. Unfortunately, it is challenging to convince someone to join you in a "knobbie," especially strangers.

There is so much crap on the Internet that I find myself frequently thinking, "I didn't need to see that."

---

1. What is your experience with technology?

2. How does it make you feel if others are using it and you are not?

3. What are the most useful applications for the novice: Email? Social Media? Photos? Search engines (Google)? Word processing? Genealogy?

4. How can technology facilitate communication and establish connections with others?

5. How can technology help you identify nonsense news and fact check information?

6. How can you avoid marketeers and scammers?

7. Can you become hooked on the Internet? Can you turn into an online pest?

8. How do you obtain technical support without being a pest?

9. Have you ever Googled yourself?

CLOSING COMMENTS:

A technological evolution is not for everyone, but in today's world most people communicate online. You can influence, entertain, and support those you care about through online connections. At some point, you may be the one person a troubled person turns to at a critical time because you are accessible online.

Computer classes customized for older people are available at libraries, colleges, and senior facilities. To avoid being overwhelmed, narrow the scope of how you use technology to those things that bring value. You don't have to follow trends and do everything the digital world offers.

Don't let the complexities and the *noise* on the Internet distract or intimidate you. Sign up. Seek a techno adventure. It will be frustrating, but it will give you a voice. And the older you get the more electronic channels of communication have to offer.

The digital world is a powerful deterrent to isolation. It has the potential to enhance your passions, give you a sense of purpose, and assure your relevance. Try going kicking and screaming into the world of technology. Do it for yourself and for others.

Technology is my window to the world, but it is also a maddening frustration.

Chapter 10

PASSION, PURPOSE, AND BLISS

Discovering what you were born to do.

Passion reflects who you are, how you see the world, and how others see you. When people ask what you do, it may seem inadequate to respond "I'm retired." You may be tempted to make something up, such as "I'm training for the Olympics." You do this to be interesting because being retired is, in itself, not interesting.

People revel in the freedom of not working for the first few years after retirement. The haunting sense of time marching by that weighs so heavily on working people fades, and it seems as if time were melting. This is heavenly, but without a passion, a person can slip into a state of melancholy—the old "Is this all there is?" mentality normally associated with a midlife crisis. Some people live their entire lives in that mode, which is okay if it makes them happy. However, most people need something more.

By moving beyond coasting into the realm of passion, a phenomenal third trimester of life is possible. Passion defeats discontent and the sense of merely taking up space. Passion produces a luscious, seductive, stimulating experience—bliss.

> *Passion* is **something you do** that causes time to go by and you don't notice. Sharing passion promotes a *sense of purpose.*

> *Bliss* is **a state of being** that happens in the now, such as holding a sleeping baby, being attacked by a litter of puppies, hearing a favorite song, or reveling in a passion.

When you find passion, you are doing what you were born to do—that which is compatible with your innate capabilities. Nothing else is needed to define you. You are enough just by *being.*

Passion is expressed without sacrifice. It is the primary driver of a sense of well-being. Once discovered, it's something you *have* to do because it fills you up. Passion makes worrisome, negative thoughts seem trivial. It murders depression and sparks feelings of bliss.

Passion doesn't have to be something of imposing scale. Don't let other people's grand passions diminish your own. It is simply what fulfills you and lights you up. Perhaps it is as elementary as building outlandish blanket forts with grandchildren or playing a musical instrument. What is more important than shaping the lives of young people or music?

Sharing a new passion keeps you from being one of those old people who tell the same old stories over and over again because they don't have anything interesting going on in the present.

Even as the relentless consequences of aging march across the body and mind, a new passion is waiting to be discovered, one that will save you from the emptiness of the present. Passion can fill you up, set you on fire, and cause you to glow. When that happens, you become a beacon.

You will know you've found a passion when you think you've done something for an hour and discover you've done it for several. Purpose materializes when your passion is shared. And then, there is this thing called bliss.

The two most important days in your life are the day you were born and the day you figured out why. . .Mark Twain

My nineties were the most productive years of my life. . .Harry Bernstein

Your value is not so much about what you did as it is about what you are doing now.

I slept and dreamt that life was joy. I awoke and saw that life was service. I acted and behold, service was joy. . .Rabindranath Tagore

Passion is where the magic resides. It's the path to mattering. It reveals unique talents and releases them to the world.

I was running—running to nothing and nowhere. My life was empty. I had no passion.

If you live in the past and that's all you talk about, you peaked early. You are boring people. You need passion.

Once you recognize within yourself a hunger for something beyond just continuing, once you taste even the possibility of touching the meaning in your life, you can never be completely content with just going through the motions. . .Oriah Mountain Dreamer, from The Invitation

Some people never experience the hunger that drives passion. They unconsciously spiral down and become old too soon. I was there once. I was killing time, and it was dying hard. I'm not there anymore. I am hungry.

My passion is fun. If I can't light up a room, I will do something wacko. Fun—it's gonna happen.

My passion is butter brickle premium ice cream. Oh wait, that's an addiction.

My passion is my grandbaby's tummy, my happy place.

I have a passion for wine. Some very fine grapes gave up their lives for wine. I feel an obligation to enjoy it. I also have a passion for cheese. Knowing some very fine cows or goats gave up. . .never mind.

———————————

1. **To what extent does retirement influence the need to find your own personal passion?**

2. **How do you find purpose? Can it come from sharing passion?**

3. **Does passion have to be something grand and all-consuming? Can it be something as simple as being a good grandparent or making each interaction with others a positive experience?**

4. **How can you share your passion?**

5. **Can you have more than one passion?**

6. **How does experiencing passion, purpose, and bliss influence others?**

———————————

CLOSING COMMENTS:

Each person has their own set of unique, innate qualities and talents that make them special. Some attributes are valued more by society than others, but each and every one is a gift. When honed and shared, the capabilities you possess are a blessing to the universe. Don't underestimate what you have to offer. Playing to your strengths is how you claim your birthright.

For many people, their work is their passion. When that is gone, a new one is waiting to be discovered. To find it, identify innate talents. Ask yourself what you loved to do as a child before the world got in the way. The retrospective life review required to write your life story can reveal aptitudes abandoned somewhere along the way.

Another way to find passion is through learning. College freshmen often discover their major by determining which courses they excel in and enjoy. When pursuing learning opportunities, you will discover a subject that lights your fire. The challenge is to figure out how to use that passion for the benefit of others.

Here is an example of a person finding his passion and sharing it. He discovered a sense of purpose that changed the lives of others and brought him bliss:

Jim was initially bummed about having to move into senior housing. However, the new environment turned out to be a blessing. Without the distractions of day-to-day living required by his previous life, he switched his focus to making life softer for others.

The financial arrangement with a senior housing facility allowed him to fix his cost of living for the rest of his life. This made it possible for him to share the remaining resources. He financed a family reunion at a wonderful resort, and paid off a mortgage for his son. He also paid off the student loan for a grandchild and set up college funds for others.

Jim learned to use a computer and put out a monthly family newsletter. He sent encouraging and humorous messages to family and friends. He wrote his life story and documented family history.

When people he knew died, he wrote to their families. His letters were rich with fascinating stories that would have otherwise been lost forever.

Although Jim was no computer whiz, he was soon showing other old folks how to use community computers at the senior center. He helped them produce life stories, which could be given as Christmas presents or as gifts at their birthday celebrations.

His efforts were so popular that he couldn't keep up with the demand, so he rallied the staff at the senior center to recruit community volunteers to assist with these endeavors. The computer center bustled with activity. A charity supplied more computers, and a local business owner gave the seniors a discount on printing. These activities were so successful, that other senior centers adopted similar programs.

Jim found his passion. Time passed by unnoticed and bliss blossomed for him and others.

Years later, when Jim was gone, others carried on his mission. Through his passion, he produced a robust legacy. Contrast this with how life would have been for him and others if he had decided to coast.

Magic is generated by nurturing the flames of passion—no matter the circumstances. Even dying can be done with passion and purpose. Go *beyond* aging well. Find your passion, embrace the purpose and bliss it generates, and share them with others.

It's never too late to do what you were born to do.

Chapter 11

ENLIGHTENMENT IS THE CAKE— SHARING IT IS THE FROSTING

When you learn something new, the brain builds new connections, and that reshuffles the deck.

Learning is not just for the young. Through continuous learning and sharing what is learned, you become a beacon in the darkness of ignorance—a player. To realize your potential, you must always be learning. A state of melancholy is incompatible with learning, so by seeking enlightenment, a sense of just going through the motions of life is avoided. Also, when you become a seeker, others cannot manipulate you.

If you stop seeking as you age, you may end up in the shallow haze of discontent or even in a state of depression. You cannot be a beacon to others in that mode. Many older people fail to appreciate the positive effect continuous learning has on themselves—and on others. Learning generates influences beyond ones self.

> This question was asked in a survey of participants in an educational program for people over sixty: What did you get out of the courses?
> Respondents revealed many benefits to themselves but missed the value of their influence as role models. Through continuous learning, they demonstrated to others that learning never ends. They also lacked awareness of the power knowledge has when it is shared.

Demonstrating that you are still learning and sharing what is learned may be the most valuable outcomes of the learning process.

Almost every college and university has a lifelong learning program for older people. Topics range from hobbies to academics. Costs are normally minimal. Some institutions offer tuition-free college courses for seniors. Interacting with young students in this setting will renew your faith in the future. And, if you are upbeat and generous with your wisdom without being preachy, your presence in the classroom will give young students an appreciation for older people. The first few days they will wonder, *Who is that old man in the back of the room?* Before long, they will be valuing that old man's input.

Learning is tricky because the world has been invaded by biased sources that distribute nonsense information under the guise of news. The Internet and talk radio have exacerbated this situation. You were brought up in an era when news was real. Now both the source and the content of news are questionable.

Much news is not news. It is commentary or outright propaganda. Sold as fact, it's designed to influence people to act against their own best interests. Through distorted information, self-serving leaders turn their followers into judgmental robots. The goal of these manipulators is to define other people's views for them. They're experts at doing so. Their motivation is power and greed.

There are sources that aspire to deliver solid, objective news. They don't tout objectivity. To them, it's a given—it goes without saying. On the other end of the spectrum are manipulators who encourage people to judge and disrespect anyone who sees the world differently than they do. Determined to push their agenda, such exploiters label all other sources of information as biased and insist that they are the only reliable source. Once they've accomplished that, they influence through fear and hate. They own you.

An all-day marathon of watching fear-based, politically-biased news influenced my psyche, and not in a good way. Nightmares followed. Ethiopian men with lariats riding mythical beasts pursued me. I got arrested at the Trinidad airport for stealing gum. On a sinking boat in the Bay of Fundy, I saw my ex-husband swimming toward me. After something bad happened in a Turkish jail and the stock market crashed, I awoke in a cold sweat. Then the horror of being Vice President occurred to me. To recover, I had to eat Funky Monkey ice cream.

As people age, they tend to see the world through the filtered lens of apprehension. This makes them susceptible to manipulation through fear, which introduces judgment and discrimination. That, in turn, leads to hate. If you are bummed or excessively angry, it may be because you are listening to biased news sources and negative commentary cleverly designed to induce fear.

When people associate closely with a group, they often become immersed in "groupthink." This means they blindly embrace whatever belief or position that group's leaders espouse on *every* issue, no matter how absurd. Otherwise reasonable people will believe anything when in the throes of "groupthink." Why?

A basic tribal need causes people to seek leaders and to rally around them—to follow. Out of loyalty to those leaders they abandon independent thought and rational judgment to support whatever positions their leaders suggest. Leaders who are self-serving seekers of power, money, or attention, are focused on what is best for them, not you. If you blindly follow them, you are being had.

Here is how shrewd media pontificators manipulate. They take a nugget of truth and build distorted, fear-based information around it. Because there is that nugget of truth in there somewhere, people accept all related information as true as well, even when it is not. Negative catch phrases and key words are repeated over and over to sell the position.

Since people are susceptible to information that supports what they already believe, the messages are framed around those beliefs. This is a brilliant, manipulative strategy. The winners in this scenario are the manipulators. Everyone else loses.

When a group criticizes another group for doing the same thing they are doing, a learned person must conclude that something is off. When a group defends their rights by stomping on the rights of others, something is off. It is like someone is playing "I Left My Heart in San Francisco" on the piano while a singer is singing "My Way." Something is off.

If you don't make an effort to seek and learn, you will appear foolish to informed, rational-thinking individuals. These enlightened people may well be your friends, children, and grandchildren. Wouldn't you rather be a wise, informed, insightful old sage than an old fool?

Embrace enlightenment. Continuously learn. Understand the motives of sources. Don't underestimate your ability to analyze facts and evidence, to interpret them, and to draw your own conclusions. Be a learned, discerning, astute older person who is a player still. Be that person.

———————————

*Learn as though you will live forever. . .*Gandhi

When someone has the need to define what they say as no spin, I look for the spin. When someone claims everyone else is biased, I look for their bias.

Facts are news. Opinions are spin. When I buy off on spin, I know I'm being played like a fine guitar.

Much of today's commentary consists of dicey deductions so irrational that it is as if someone is dotting the t's and crossing the small j's. The amazing thing is that some people don't even notice.

The insanity of discourse can cloud what is true—that we are all part of the same universe. There are no "others." Still, some people are alive because it is against the law to kill them. (I can't believe I said that. . .There are no others. There are no others. There are no others.)

I refuse to be influenced by people sitting around on yachts wondering what the poor people are doing.

Someone began reporting information so ridiculous and shocking that it was as though a body had sat up in a coffin. I spoke up, not to change their opinion, but to make certain they knew I had a different one.

When I don't challenge nonsensical discourse, the persons delivering it assume I agree with them. I won't allow them to conclude that I support their position because I didn't speak up. So I speak up. I do so by asking questions. It's entertaining to observe them trying to rationalize the absurd.

Befuddled by the trend toward hate and polarization fueled by distorted information, I feel like the kid who heard an echo and wondered how it knew what to say.

Someone is boring me. I think it's me. . . .Dylan Thomas

When someone says something totally ridiculous, my sarcastic nature kicks in. I say, "You are so-o-o-o deep."

My response to negative nonsense is, "I believe you believe that, but I don't."

Right fighters have to be right. Do you want to be right or do you want to be happy?. . .Dr. Phil

I'll tell you what I think, if that's okay. If not, I'll tell you anyway. . .Grandma

---

1. Does the value of knowledge increase as physical capability declines or does it lose significance?

2. What are lucrative venues for learning?

3. How can you apply what you learn? Share it?

4. How do you cope with disturbing news?

5. How do you identify distorted information sources? How can information be vetted?

6. What role does "groupthink" play in how you take in information?

7. Why do so many people look to others to interpret information for them?

8. How can you confront distorted information? What kind of questions can you ask to expose the motives of sources of biased rhetoric?

9. How can Internet social networking be managed to shut out disturbing messaging?

CLOSING COMMENTS:

To avoid being a pawn in the theater of news, remember this: Every source has an agenda. For some that is to intentionally distort information for their own purposes. Speak out against nonsense. Other people might buy off on the distortion. Be smarter than that. It's a challenge to reason with those who embrace the unreasonable, but speak up. *Your silence when someone advocates malarky is interpreted by that person as endorsement.* Is that the message you want to send? You don't have to argue, just make it clear you do not agree.

On your aging journey, consider the concept of "groupthink" and how you want to relate to it. Do you want to develop opinions based on facts, solid sources, and logical analysis? If so, you will land on both sides of the political spectrum because your opinions will be derived issue by issue, not by what you are told to think. If you don't do this, you may become a pawn and a victim. You cannot be an effective leader for your family in that mode.

No group or person is so special that they have all the answers. Ask yourself: Are they really experts, or are they puffers and impostors? Why would you let them think for you? Here is the defining question: Do they make money or gain power by convincing you and others to embrace their convictions?

You don't need someone to translate facts for you. You are capable of interpreting them yourself. Those focused on manipulating others aspire to be your single source of information. They do not desire an evidence-based society, and critical thinking is their enemy. Watch out for slanted rhetoric wrapped around facts and manipulators who use your core values to distract you from other important issues.

Just because you or someone else thinks something in their head, does not make it a fact. It is a thought. To challenge those who embrace the unreasonable, you don't have to argue. You can say, "I'm sorry if the facts don't line up with your narrative." Or ask questions. When they masterfully change the subject by throwing up decoys (introducing distracting points that support their rhetoric), ask the question again. And again.

When you ignore evidence and facts and cease independent thinking, you enter a place where manipulators own you. By engaging in continuous learning and assuming the perspective of a healthy skeptic, you can challenge slanted rhetoric.

Be a seeker, a gatherer of facts, and an astute interpreter of information. Consider the motives of sources. Engage in continuous learning. Learn how propaganda and group think work. Show others the value of being an informed, wise old soul. Share your wisdom. When you do so, you keep your power and your reputation as a discerning person.

> *A lot of news today is not news. It is commentary, or possibly even propaganda. Knowing how to fact check is vital to your sanity and to your standing with rational thinkers, which most likely includes your grandchildren.*

Chapter 12

GRUMPY OR GRATEFUL—A CHOICE

It is not happiness that makes you grateful.
It is gratefulness that makes you happy. . .
Brother David Steindle-Rast

Attitude defines the present and predicts the future. You cannot be perpetually grumpy and be connected to others. People will shut you out. Grumpy old people are ungrateful and resourceful at discovering tidbits of experience over which to ruin their lives. Their complaints are tragically predictive of unfortunate outcomes.

Fascination with the downside of life has consequences. Vicious cycles of fatalism hover like angry poltergeists. A grumpy person becomes old too soon and drags others into the abyss of negativity. Contrast that with living in a way that enhances the lives of others. You inspire or distresses others by your *way of being* in the world.

A man in line at the airport observed an agent repeatedly harangued by passengers unhappy about a cancelled flight. When it was his turn, he handed his boarding pass to the agent and said, "I'm sorry you had to endure all that. Do with me what you will." A smile crossed the agent's face as he booked the man on another flight and handed him a First Class boarding pass.

By how you live daily, you have the potential to have a positive or negative impact on others. The gap between these two behaviors is huge. How you drive, treat clerks in stores, look at people, greet them, open doors for them, or whatever other interaction you experience, makes a difference. Everything about you sends a message. *It is impossible to be a neutral influence.*

Some influences are subtle, although their importance should not be underestimated. Others are blatant, as in this situation:

Wilber, a prickly old fellow in slippers, reclined in an overstuffed chair capable of throwing him out of it with the push of a button. He groused about one thing after another, causing his niece, Madelyn, who was visiting him, to assume his aura was ecru. Wilber summed up his opinions, "I don't like nobody." He contemplated his next reflection, and then said, "And I don't like dogs." *Well, okay*, Madelyn mused, noting the Beagle nestled beside him in his chair.

Wilber's wrinkled, squished-up face reflected his cantankerous nature as he pondered his next observation. His niece speculated he was going to tell her how much he hated puppies, or teddy bears, or babies. Instead, he moved on to a testy comment about the weather.

Madelyn interjected a more positive topic, but Wilber hijacked the tactic with his next comment. "I don't like morning people. . .or mornings. . .or people."

Later, as she departed, Madelyn said, "Have a nice day, Wilber," to which he responded, "I have other plans."

Madelyn left marveling at how Wilber had successfully sucked the life out of her in short order. He put so much serious negativity out into the world, that she concluded Wilber was afraid. Very afraid.

There are two basic emotions that drive behavior: fear and love. Which one is embraced determines whether a person is grumpy or grateful. Grumpiness promotes fear and isolation while gratefulness fosters cheerfulness and connections.

Fear pushes people into the victim mode. Their fears and aggravations torment them. This, in turn, causes them to view others as persecutors. An unfortunate loop materializes as these tortured souls respond to their perceived persecution by persecuting others with their negative spirits.

People like Wilber gravitate to the negative and are quick to embrace pessimistic information. They seek out sources that deliver it. Threads of meanness flow through their dialogue. When in victim mode, a vicious cycle of fear and anger is promoted. Fear is invasive, and anger destructive. Unhappiness is inevitable in this circumstance, and the anger breeds hate. What makes some people hate so hard? Fear.

It's amazing how creative prickly people can be about discovering ways to sabotage their lives. Here is an example of a grumpy guy. What do you predict will be the outcome of the following scenario?

> In a job interview an interviewer asked, "What is your greatest weakness?"
> The applicant responded, "I'm too honest."
> "That doesn't seem like a weakness."
> "I don't give a crap what you think."

Crankiness can be humorous, but how would you like to work with that guy? You get to choose your frame of mind.

> A teenage boy bumped into an older woman in a store and said, "Sorry, granny." Such an incident could be interpreted by the woman as either

insulting or humorous. If she observed the kid for a while, she would most likely find him a charming, entertaining mess. By viewing the boy as a mother's beloved son and someone's adored grandson, she sees him as the jewel he is.

Grumpiness is a choice. You can always find something to grouch about—bad drivers, hyped-up young folks, nuisance neighbors, health issues, lost remotes, noisy restaurants, hearing aids, and complicated inventions. Such things invade your world and make you grumpy—or not.

Being grateful and connecting with others in a positive way sparks happiness. Conversely, relating to merchants of fear and romancing the negative promotes disillusionment, angst, anger, judgement, a sour disposition, and loneliness. Unhappiness is inevitable under this scenario. Why would you choose that?

I'm guilty. Gripe, gripe, gripe, and that's on a good day.

When people gripe, I interrupt them and ask, "How can I help?" That is unless they are complaining about constipation.

I knew if I lived long enough this would happen.

There is always something to be upset about, but very few things are worthy of that response.

When a driver pulls out in front of me, rather than thinking, "What an idiot," I think, "I did that once." I'm thankful it wasn't me who did it this time. If a driver gives me an angry look, I don't get mad. I think, "Get on with your big bad self." I'm just grateful I can still drive.

Sometimes I have to decide whether to watch the news or to remain sane.

I was watching someone who was watching someone doing something stupid on television. I thought about how easily the observer was amused. Then it occurred to me that I was watching someone who was watching someone doing something stupid.

Surround sound makes me want to kill my husband. Instead, I do our taxes in the tool shed.

I have a headphone contraption that can effectively block out a Guns and Roses concert.

It helps my disposition to interpret hustle and bustle as energy—a buzzing around in which I don't have to participate but at the center of which I can live.

Aging can have the weight of granite or the wings of an eagle.

It is tempting to be seduced into a constant state of medical tests and treatments. I could go to the doctor every day. If I did so, I would surely be grumpy.

———————————

1. **What are the primary drivers of grumpy behavior? Why do some people respond to situations by being grumpy and others do not?**

2. **Is it possible to decide whether to be grumpy?**

3. **Is acceptance an antidote for grumpiness?**

4. **What role does being grateful play in keeping you from becoming grumpy?**

5. **What coping techniques keep you from being grumpy? Does an "oh well" perspective help?**

6. **How can the victim mode be avoided when bad things happen?**

7. **How do you respond to grumpy people? What if they are your partner?**

8. **How do medical treatments and health conditions affect disposition? Does grumpiness promote excessive medical care, drug use, and bad habits?**

———————————

CLOSING COMMENTS:

If grumpiness or gratefulness is a choice, it must be a simple matter of choosing to be grateful. But old age is a severe master; challenges are profound. When you fail at this—and you will—forgive yourself and carry on. Your ability to recover and cope is influenced by your concept of self. Consider this:

You are braver than you believe,
stronger than you seem, and
smarter than you think. . . .Christopher Robin

A way to avoid being seduced into grumpiness is to seek fun in unusual circumstances:

Buzz was irritated that his grandson wore his pants so low his underwear showed. Rather than gripe about it, he persuaded relatives to wear low-slung pants with underwear revealed to a family dinner—an intervention of sorts. Children, women, and old folks waddled around with pant crotches almost to their knees. Baby diapers were even riding low. This was a hoot. Pictures were taken, memories made, and a grumpy episode of lectures and disapproval was replaced with fun and laughter.

It is likely your best hope for being grateful and enjoying life involves a grandchild or other small person. A treasure trove of quirky interpretations and gleeful responses to the simplest things come from these tiny creatures. How they view you is related to your disposition. If they are staring at you like a tree full of owls, you might be scaring them. If they adore you, nothing is better than that.

A grandma dropped her three-year-old granddaughter off at day care for the first time. The teacher asked the little girl if this was her grandma. Since the family always called the grandma GoGo, the question puzzled the girl. Finally, she said, "No, she's my girlfriend."

Grandparenting is grand, but it presents challenges. Here is one grandparent's experience.

After spending the good part of an hour with my sidekick hiding in a cardboard box that smelled like, well, like cardboard and after performing a chemistry experiment with Fruit Loops, I found myself playing an alphabet game and trains at the same time (we were multi-tasking). While trying to determine if a letter was a *big W* or a *big M*, I had an out-of-body experience. Floating near the ceiling, I observed myself saying, "Come on over here *little s*, and *big R*, you need to scoot over there," as a train circled my butt. Pondering the letters *little d* and *little b* didn't help matters. I came back to reality when a squeaky voice complained that my butt was blocking Thomas the Train. "Well, E-x-c-u-s-e m-e," I replied with my best Steve Martin inflection. He rolled around laughing and pounding the floor. So did I. At dinner that evening when his mother insisted he not put peas in his milk, he said, "Well, E-x-c-u-s-e M-e."

Another solution for grumpiness is the *oh well* concept suggested earlier. It encourages acceptance of things you cannot control. This releases you to focus on the issues you can. One of those solutions is the choice whether to respond with grumpiness or gratefulness when frustrated.

Do not assume it is human ecology to be grumpy when you are old. Being grumpy is aging disrespectfully. Shine and sparkle. Each day offers opportunities to disempower the demons that drag you down. Grumpy or grateful? Your choice.

You get to choose your way of being in the world.

Chapter 13

THE EBB AND FLOW OF AGING

Sometimes we just try too hard.

On the slippery slope of aging, anger comes in gentle ripples. You can cope with this emotion by applying a rationalization: When something is lost, something else is gained. Or perhaps you apply a dose of acceptance through a simple *oh well.*

These coping mechanisms work fairly well. However, when anger comes in smashing waves that wash over you and drag you down in an undertow, a more potent strategy is required, one that produces a rally—a retreat from the abyss. This strategy comes in the form of *surrender.*

Sometimes we just try too hard. You can't reason your way out of every downturn. It's occasionally acceptable to give up the fight, to surrender to the downturn, sink into the depths of despair, and wallow in misery. There's a catch, though. You must do this only for a day.

Surrendering to a downturn acknowledges vulnerability as an important emotion. Because of the natural ebb and flow of life, you can sink into that vulnerability knowing a rally is inevitable the next day. Even if you don't orchestrate it yourself, the universe will deliver salvation through daily increments of time. This fabulous feature is the universe showing off.

Here is a scenario that portrays the ebb and flow of aging. This story reveals the absurdity of a bad day and the value of surrendering to it:

My mind is foggy. I have to check the computer to determine it is Wednesday. I go to the mailbox twice, and I can't find my slippers or my scissors.

Anxieties accumulate and the cloud of a terminal illness raises its ugly head: *There is something wrong with my body. I don't know what it is, but something is wrong. I just know it.*

I contemplate my body. *There must be a tumor the size of a soccer ball in my stomach. That pain in my hip, it's probably bone cancer. The brown spot on my leg—melanoma. The ache in my back —a heart condition. The headache—an impending stroke. There are ridges in a toenail. I don't know what that means, but it's surely a sign of something awful.*

I access the Mayo Clinic website and input an array of symptoms. *Oh, my god! I'm gonna die!*

After exhausting my bad day "go to" solutions—chocolate and bacon—I decide to go to bed early, but I'm too upset to sleep. So I take a sleeping pill. It sticks in my throat, which requires that I eat everything in the kitchen to try to get it down, calories I don't need. Irritating and distracting, the pill remains embedded. *When will it finally go down? Will it cause me to oversleep and miss Judge Judy and Dr. Phil tomorrow?*

Finally, I give up. Sweet surrender. Although I am most likely dying, I fall into the haze of sleep. The next morning I awake with the morning light streaming in, birds chirping, and soft sheets and blankets surrounding me. I didn't die.

Then the rally. Acknowledging the ebb and flow, I do what I do every morning. It is habit. I concentrate on gratefulness. *I am blessed to have this day, to know it is Thursday, to live in a wonderful nest, and to have the freedom to choose to do today those things that make me happy.*

After acknowledging that the day is a gift and embracing the new beginning it bestows, I consider how to be useful this day, whether in a small way or a large one. With that, I say to myself, *Sign me up for another day—a better day. Screw the prospect of a crisis. I am going to take today. It is mine. I own this day. I am on fire.* With that, the devil says, "Oh, crap, she's back, and she knows it's Thursday."

Surrendering might seem counter intuitive. In general, it makes more sense to fight the good fight and overcome. But when lying on the couch in cuddly pajamas, backstroking to reach the Cheetos and bubblegum flavored jelly beans doesn't reverse a downturn, surrender might be the cure.

It's okay to be broken for a day. This releases anxiety and postures you for a fresh start the next day. However, do this *only* for an increment of time. A day is an ideal timeframe in which to flounder and work despair and anger out of your system.

(This strategy applies only to temporary downturns. If you find yourself in a continuous funk, seek professional help. Depression is treatable, and you deserve peace of mind and a peaceful heart.)

I searched for my glasses only to discover while in the shower that I was wearing one pair and had the backup pair on my head. This caused me to suggest to my children that they put me in a home, to which one responded, "Fine. As long as it isn't mine."

More and more often I pretend to hear when I don't. This is isolating and causes me to say stupid, irrelevant things that make no sense, such as "Chocolate also does that."

When I watch television with my children, they ask me to turn it down. I say, "WHAT?"

Having a bad day, I forgot the forgiveness crap and messed with a caller, an ex-husband. I justified my behavior on the supposition that he deserved a piece of Karma pie. However, my actions were really motivated by revenge and the fear that something inside of me might break—again.

Guilty about my hateful state, I focused on positive thoughts like: I didn't glue my fingers together today.

My shoulders slump, my tummy pooches out, my chin drops—and I don't care. It is a sad, sorry situation when you don't care if your tummy pooches out.

When I thought the day could not get worse, the person driving ahead of me squirted water on his windshield. It sprayed back onto mine. I felt abused. I wished I had him in my passenger seat in 100 degree weather. A seat warmer can be a weapon.

*Everyone is scared on the inside. Don't compare your inside to someone else's outside. . .*Anne Lamott

---

1. Is it okay to occasionally sink into the depths of despair? How do you keep a period of surrender from becoming a permanent condition?

2. What do you do when you surrender? Eat? Sleep? Do whatever feels good?

3. What can you do to snap yourself out of a sobering downturn?

4. What do you do if you feel down for an extended period of time?

5. What is the difference between down time and clinical depression? If you feel depression creeping in, should you reveal that to others?

6. How do you keep your down experiences from affecting others negatively?

7. Are your *down* episodes funny in retrospect?

8. How does surrender fit into acceptance of the natural ebb and flow of life?

CLOSING COMMENTS:

Aging can be awful or wildly wonderful, and it changes from day to day, sometimes minute to minute. In a downturn, when anger flares and thrusts you into an emotional abyss, acknowledge the ebb and flow. Know that there is good to come.

When drowning in an ocean of misery, give yourself a visa for a day trip of blazing self-pity, misguided fear, angry resignation, bacon, Snickers, or whatever else makes it all better. It's okay to occasionally surrender for a day.

The beauty of a day-long crash is that you can do it without sucking anyone else into the muck. Make it your personal journey. Taste it, and move on.

Another way to look at hard times is illustrated by a high school teacher concerned about suicide among teens.

A teacher drew a line across all the whiteboards in the classroom. She erased about a two inch area on that line, and said to her students, "This line is your life. This little blank space is high school. So what if you aren't popular now. So what if you don't get invited to prom. So what if your childhood was miserable. You've got the whole rest of your life ahead of you after high school. You get to call the shots and make smart choices."

A downturn is a small increment of time when considering your entire lifeline. When hit after hit takes you down, remember that, although it is a bad time, a rally is around the corner. When things are at their worst, they are bound to get better.

Life is made up of peaks and valleys. They are exacerbated by age, but the natural ebb and flow of life, the daily increments of time—the dusk at night and the sunrise in the morning—will save you. Nothing ever stays the same, and every day is a new day. Each one proffers a fresh start.

Doing things for others will help bring you out of a downturn. Humanity is flush with need. Be a shepherd. Be everyone's champion. Be someone's wingman. Be generous. A person, determined to stay positive no matter what, developed the following affirmation, which she repeats every morning before her feet hit the floor:

> I will not be a victim. I will not torture myself or others with my issues. I will bask in gratefulness. I will share my gifts. I will soften the world for others. I will create this day and make it a masterpiece.

Go *beyond* aging well. Take advantage of the most extraordinary, underrated gift of the universe—increments of days. Embrace the ebb and flow and make the rally a *coup de triumph*. Do this for yourself and for "the others."

Don't despair. When things are at their worst,
there is no way to go but up.

Chapter 14

COPING WITH THE GRADUAL DECLINE AND SUDDENLY-ONE-MOMENT INCIDENTS

You're only as strong as your weakest part.

Look back at how you were ten years ago and how you are now. It's obvious things are going downhill. Even if you want to donate a kidney, no one wants it. The goal to "not fall down" takes precedence over more exciting prospects. The future hints at a sequence of minor events that build until a trigger is flipped, and reality slaps you—hard: You are a ticking time bomb.

A woman believed her mind was transitioning into something similar to swiss cheese, so she began taking a memory enhancing herb. She said, "I

only take half doses because I don't want
to remember everything."

She was not to the point of answering the
door after knocking on wood, nor did she
send Christmas cards in July. She hadn't
gotten a perm and then got another the next
day. She wasn't putting toothpaste in the
refrigerator or car keys in the sugar bowl.
She hadn't tried to bake cookies in the
dishwasher. But she did believe people
living in her attic stole her slippers, hid the
remote, and ate her last PayDay candy bar.
She was dealing with mental consequences
of *the gradual decline.*

In addition to mental influences, a litany of
minor physical incidents expose older folks to
troubling signs of *the gradual decline.*

A man swatted at gnats flying
around his head. One lit on his shirt. He
slapped it, but it returned. Turns out the
gnat invasion was floaters in his eyes,
little nuisance specks that moved around
like UFOs.

To treat her arthritis, a woman wore
a magnet bracelet so powerful that
kitchen utensils stuck to it.

A lady was a seasoned multi-tasker.
She could cough, sneeze, laugh, and
pee at the same time.

If you live long enough, such things as
eyebrows thinning, a larger shoe size, dents in the
nose from reading glasses, and the fact that the only
dance you can do anymore is the Macarena are in
your future. A dietician's diet causes you to speculate
that he trained at Guantanamo Bay. It's not unusual for
you to carry teeth around in your purse. The loss of
hearing, vision, and other physical and mental
capabilities introduces shifts in how you function.

Such degradation is a challenge every older
person faces to some degree. How you respond to this
barrage creates positive or negative energy. You can
be an inspiring old person *no matter what happens*, or
you can become a looming presence.

In addition to the abundance of mental and
physical challenges, there are pesky cosmetic
changes, which shouldn't be important, but they are.
As Nora Ephron said, "If you could see your elbows,
you would kill yourself."

You can romance your stomach all you want,
chances are you are not going to love it or change it.
At some point, your body begins to make the same
noises as a coffeemaker. (A man had a brilliant
explanation for grandchildren when such noises
occurred. He said, "I stepped on a duck." The kids

adopted this explanation to the astonishment of their parents and teachers.)

In contrast to the *gradual decline*, a *suddenly-one-moment incident* involves an event that changes everything in an instant. If you have not experienced one yet, brace yourself. You may no longer be vulnerable to injuring yourself from a rock under a Slip 'N Slide, but you are at risk for hurting yourself walking on a sidewalk. You are one fall—one broken hip—away from the harsh reality of a major medical experience and possibly a continuous care facility.

> A woman in the hospital was told she needed a pacemaker, which she refused. A friend asked her why. She responded, "It makes me feel old."
>
> Her friend said, "You are old. I'm old, thank God. Would you want to go back to being young? Really? Do you want to relive any of that? Maybe there were a few high points, but you know some real crap surrounded them. Come on, girlfriend. Get that pacemaker, and let's go to Italy."

You can't reframe aging if you don't accept it. If you can't see the good in everything, you are like a cat scratching around on linoleum instead of seeking a litter box. There is no denying that being one health crisis away from a downward spiral can be tragically distracting from life. To go *beyond* aging well, you must stare down the fear of that unpredictable, imminent crisis moment that changes everything—a moment you know is in your future or that of someone you care about. You must live life full out in spite of—or because of—this prospect.

A powerful coping strategy for scary situations involves examining the worst-case scenario and developing a plan for dealing with it. Once that is done, the future is not so intimidating.

A man's company was failing. He was stressed over financial worries. It was a good job, and he lived well. That was slipping away. A friend suggested he explore the worst-case scenario and determine if he could live with that. His friend asked, "Could you live in a more modest house like your parents and drive a nondescript car and be happy?"

The man determined he could. In fact, even if he never had another high-paying job he could live better than his parents, and they did fine. With this perspective—the worst-case scenario— the cloud of anxiety lifted. He was free of the fear that had enveloped him.

Most older people's worst-case scenarios involve much more disturbing experiences: running out of money, suffering a painful terminal illness, being a burden to others, ending up in a nursing home, and losing one's mind. That's a nasty list of outcomes. You must contemplate them in order to develop a plan to address them. It is this plan that has the potential to be a comfort to yourself and others.

Michael J. Fox suggests that one not focus on worst-case scenarios because if they happen, you have lived them twice. Makes sense, but you can bet he has a plan. Most likely, he developed it and then went on with living. All indications are that he is at peace with his precarious future.

It is amazing what a fresh perspective and a plan can do. Be brave. By contemplating the scenarios you dread most and developing plans to deal with them, you can get on with living.

When you are young, mental and medical crises are not on your radar. With maturity, you learn to ruin your life with anticipation.

Lying in a stairwell one day after a fall, I wondered, "Is this it—the moment that changes everything?" Fortunately, it wasn't, but it could have been. I know where I'm headed. When that event does happen, and I can't do something anymore, I plan to focus on something else I can do.

When I see a restroom sign, I say, "Well, I might as well pee while I'm here."

The doctor wanted to test me for Gerd. I told him, "I'm not having Gerd. I'm just not."

Focus on yourself—mind, body, and spirit. Choose a point person for friends to contact [for updates]. This minimizes talking about your cancer and treatment all the time so, instead, you can focus on your health. . .Olivia Newton-John

*I can't hear so good, can't see so good, can't walk so good, and I am no good. I'm madder than an old wet hen. . .*Mom

I am a pragmatic realist. Believing everything happens for a reason doesn't work for me. I'm okay with accepting that "things just happen." I require no explanations beyond coincidence.

When I discovered my new doctor's office was full of Elvis paraphernalia, I got all shook up.

I have a code for my daughter when I need help. I say, "Black Hawk down."

My nurse showed up with a rectal thermometer above her ear. I inquired, "Where's your pencil?"

I asked my doctor, "What's wrong with my hearing?" He said, "You can't hear."

I wear a phone earpiece so I can talk to myself in public places. People assume I'm on the phone.

My wife told me if I got so bad that I started to wander, she was going to open the door and let me out.

I asked my husband, "Will you feed me Jello if I'm sick?" He said, "I'd tell you to wait till that stuff melts, and you can suck it up through a straw while I watch this here hockey game."

When I fall down, I say, "I meant to do that."

I learned not to eat inferno chimichangas.

When friends have surgery, I ask if they have drugs. If so, I ask them to give me some. I'm not a nice person.

I'm aware that I'm the target market of the for-profit medical industry.

When I came out of surgery my son asked me how I was doing. I said, "I'm 'mostly' okay."

———————————

1. **How much do those older than you influence how you deal with mental and physical decline? Do you have good role models?**

2. **Can poor role models show you what not to do?**

3. **How much should you contemplate something bad happening to you?**

4. Are people delusional when they avoid reality, or is denial a good way to cope?

5. What can you do to cope with mental lapses?

6. What strategies can you apply to deal with health and medical conditions?

7. How do you cope when those you are close to experience crises?

8. Do you have a plan for worst-case scenarios?

CLOSING COMMENTS:

Never forget how much you affect those you care about by how you react to unfortunate aging experiences—yours or someone else's. Many of these events can be interpreted as more positive than most people imagine. It is tempting to self-limit and let the downsides overshadow opportunities. I found humor in an unfortunate experience:

When physical degradation happens, I don't get too upset. I have a mantra: *work the problem*. This helped me through a nosebleed crisis necessitating a trip to the emergency room. The setting implied a guaranteed ER nightmare except for the potential for glimpses of handsome policemen, firemen, and other men in uniform who occupy those places late at night.

I drove to the hospital emergency room where I bled on the reception desk and a clipboard of requisite paperwork, which I returned to the receptionist dotted with drops of blood. Apparently, I was not ER worthy. He instructed me to have a seat in the waiting room where I waited— bleeding and scaring small children. Finally, I worked the problem and drove myself home, called an ambulance, and was whisked into the depths of ER hell.

A doctor asked me if I'd had an accident. I said, "No. I picked my nose." He and an intern stifled chuckles and knowingly looked at each other. I said, "Wh-at?" He responded, "You're the first person with a nosebleed to admit to picking your nose. Everyone picks their nose." I said, "I'm old. I have no dignity left. Why lie?"

He and the intern set to work as my mind wandered. *Have I lost more blood than the pint I would have given if I donated some? If I ever have sex again, would I or the old fellow have a nosebleed?* I didn't share these thoughts since I had enough mental capacity to edit myself. This would soon change.

While the physician set up some intimidating equipment, the intern, who resembled Keith Urban, stood beside my bed, clipboard in hand, asking me medical history questions. I answered while struggling to breathe, swallowing blood, and pinching my nose as per instructions. I responded to his questions about an ingrown toenail, the date of my tonsillectomy in 1968, and when I got my first period.

When Keith Urban asked when I had my last period, I lost my patience, which was never a redeeming quality anyway. I responded, "I'm sixty-seven years old."

Still not getting it, he asked if I was menopausal. I wanted to ask, "What part of sixty-seven do you not understand?" I considered inquiring if he still had his baby teeth, but instead I said again, "I'm sixty-seven years old." A slight smile crossed the lips of the doctor on the other side of the bed. I smiled back, both of us entertained by the innocence of the intern who looked like Keith Urban.

This distraction quickly faded and my eyes pleaded with the doctor. *Please help me.* My capacity to filter information waned. I told him and Keith Urban about an old dog named Lucy who was post menopausal and turned into a lesbian.

As I lay there, a handsome uniformed cop in the hall caused me to contemplate my feet. Having left the house in a dither, I wore slippers. Actually, I was a bit of a mess all over—sloppy clothes, bloody hands, chili on my shirt, and hair that resembled sofa stuffing. I mostly wished I'd put on nice shoes, though. My slippers looked like something an old woman would wear, one who was w-a-y past menopause.

For some reason (perhaps it was the resident resembling Keith Urban or the handsome policeman in the hallway), it occurred to me I no longer knew what I looked like naked. That was undoubtedly a good thing, but the thought and the slippers made me feel incredibly old.

On that slippery slope, I worked the problem and forced myself to focus on coping. I nestled into the bed and contemplated what color to paint my bedroom. I settled on subtle gray stripes accented with purple accessories and shiny glass objects. I couldn't wait to get to Home Depot and Z-Gallery.

The doctor instructed me to relax as he stuck a long instrument resembling a cattle prod up my nose as Keith Urban, looking good, observed. I took a deep breath and said to myself, *Work the problem, Nik. Work the problem.*

A nosebleed is a tangible problem. Many problems are made up in your head. The tactic of *fake it till you make it* is helpful when your mind drags you down. Force yourself to get out among people. Act untroubled and gleeful and soon you will feel that way. Although at first it appears you are okay when you are not, soon you are okay.

Another tactic is to deal gently with healthcare providers. A friend pitched into a nurse in a hospital and rarely saw a caretaker for the rest of her stay. Also, develop a relationship with a pharmacists and doctors. I have done so. They call me by name.

My pharmacist remembers me as a person, not a prescription. When I pick up medication, I ask questions: "Will this change the color of my eyes or interact with Jamba Juice? Are projectile vomiting and anal leakage side affects? What are the odds of involuntary movements occurring, and will they be permanent? Is it possible the seat warmer in my car caused my yeast infection?"

When pills are a different shape and color, I complain to the pharmacist, "I'm concerned these are male hormones and I'll grow a mustache."

I've told him, "I don't care what others say, I like you anyway." My pharmacist remembers me.

I ask my doctor questions like, "What happens if I eat expired yogurt?" I once suggested that trans-vaginal ultrasound was a good name for a rock band. I requested Demerol because something weird happened to my earlobes.

I asked a radiologist if he could fix my radio. My doctors remember me.

The older you get, the more intense the bombardment of issues. And personal challenges are compounded by those of others you care about.

Sometimes those losses involve death. Concentrating on how those who are gone would want you to react encourages you to move on—to not let those losses rob you of joy. People you've lost invested in you. You can't deliver a return on their investment in the depths of despair. As Alex Witchel said, "Stop worrying about who's not here and start worrying about who is."

When attitude changes, behavior changes automatically. When bad things happen—own them. Go beyond aging well. React in a way that inspires others even when you are in the throes of the gradual decline or a suddenly-one-moment incident. Make a difference by how you demonstrate your aging experience. Doing so is a gift to yourself and to others.

How do you grow old gracefully? Stay weird.

Chapter 15

TOUGH TRANSITIONS:
LET'S DO THIS THING

When need eclipses ability, you must
go someplace where aging is not a problem.
Nursing home? Hell yeah. Let's do this thing.

**If you had an anti-bucket list of things you
didn't want to experience, it would most likely
include giving up driving, using a walker or
wheelchair, or going into a continuous care facility
(a fancy name for nursing home, the most dreaded
word in the vocabularies of older people.)**

You will know when you've arrived at that
point. The parent/child relationship shifts, and people
talk about you as though you are not in the room.
This happens because you lived long enough to
experience it. Many people don't.

Anticipating transitions can produce severe
apprehension, but planning for them is paramount to

aging *beyond* well. Reality will not be denied. If you don't make the hard decisions your aging experience requires, someone else will be forced to make them for you. That is an unfair burden to place on anyone, especially those you profess to care about.

When you say *never* ("I'm *never* giving up my car." or "I'm *never* going into a nursing home."), you are ignoring reality and avoiding personal accountability. Responsibility is shifted to others. This leaves a devastating trail of inconvenience, worry, and guilt for those you are supposed to care about most. Do you really want to do that to them? This is *your* aging experience, not theirs. Own it.

At every stage of life, the proper place for a person is determined by their condition. What would it be like to feel as though you are in your place no matter where you are?

A little girl had an "air" about her from the day she was born. You could see it in her earliest photos. It was reflected in the curious, matter-of-fact way she observed people and responded to situations confidently and calmly. She assertively interacted with others (except when she met Santa Claus). Her way of being in the world projected: "I am here. I belong. *I am in my place.*"

No matter your place, no matter your path, you belong. We've all been to nursing homes and seen the people there in a terrible state, ambling down the halls and sleeping in wheelchairs in hallways. But you must know that if you have to go there, you won't be the person you are today. You will be one of those people. You will be in your place.

Life may be rough for you, but others are going down the path with you. It is possible to own your aging experience and to make tough transitions your burden, not theirs. You can say, "Let's do this thing," even if it sucks.

How do you know when it is time to make the senior housing, assisted living, or nursing home decision? When you've been lost in a mall? When you set something on fire? When you take an afternoon nap, wake up, and it is seven in the morning? When you had a moment of clarity—once? When you can't reach your feet? When you conclude pop beads are jewelry? When Ed Grimley and Terry Bradshaw are appealing? When you are inadvertently funny? When you ask the Walmart trolley driver, "Is this the bus to St. Louis?"

Viv was resolute about not letting her life intrude on those of her children. When she learned her daughter turned down a trip to Europe because she worried about leaving her mother, Viv said, "Let's do this thing." She sold her house and went into assisted living. Her daughter went on the European vacation.

Later, after falling several times and struggling with medications and daily affairs, Viv again said, "Let's do this thing" and went into a nursing home. Determined not to cause worry or to put the burden of tough decisions on others, Viv owned her aging experience. In doing so, she gave a gift.

Most older people delay tough decisions. They resist canes, walkers, and wheelchairs with a vengeance, even when those items are the path to liberation.

A handicapped lady struggled with walking but resisted using a wheelchair. She finally acquiesced, and the freedom, speed, and fluid movement her electric wheelchair provided was intoxicating.

A silver-haired speed demon, she zoomed up and down sidewalks and around halls in the senior center. Soon she was in trouble with the center's staff for speeding. "Slow down, Mario," the center manager said, "This is not Indianapolis."

After an episode of "chicken" in the hallway with another race car driver, the manager sentenced them to wheelchair purgatory until speed regulators could be installed, at which time the racers were restricted to slow-mo "chicken."

Driving is something older people cling to long after they should give it up. Will you muster the courage to initiate that sacrifice when you become a danger to yourself and others? Or will you force that decision on others and then resent them for making it? Giving up driving is a defining incident. It marks the end of independence. Not driving has benefits, though. Cars are expensive. Perhaps you can make better use of that money or use it to hire a driver. The primary advantage of not driving is that you never have to parallel park again. For the most part, driving is a hassle. Stressful and teeming with rude and careless drivers, the road requires strong coping skills. Driving can ruin your day.

An old black and white movie starring W. C. Fields illustrates an unorthodox response to the frustration of driving. Fields and his rich girlfriend, out for a Sunday drive, were repeatedly bullied by road hogs. Fed up, they purposely ran into one. This retaliatory fender bender was so rewarding that W.C. and his wealthy girlfriend bought another new car and ran into the next road hog they came across. This scenario was repeated several times throughout the day. No sane person would endorse this response, but it demonstrates how to turn a negative into a positive.

A car is a weapon. In addition to significant risks to yourself, many people will suffer considerable angst if you continue driving when you shouldn't. That is not the worst of it. The consequences can be severe —the ultimate nightmare. You could kill someone, perhaps a small child with his whole life ahead of him, or a mother with babies, or a father with a family to support. It is selfish to ignore such probabilities when your capabilities have deteriorated to the point that the risk is substantial. Is a trip to the grocery store worth that?

Another reality you will face, if you live long enough, is deteriorating health. Excessive and often unproductive medical procedures—many of them invasive, traumatic, painful, and outrageously expensive—reflect our country's for-profit healthcare system. Our cultural inability to accept the inevitable exacerbates this situation. It is important to acknowledge the reality that the medical community cannot fix everything that is wrong with your body. You don't have to accept every treatment offered.

If you live long enough, you are likely to have a rough go at some point. But you are the master of your disposition and your spirit. You've heard the expressions: *Play the cards you're dealt,* and *Bloom where you are planted.* Consider how such advice can influence your decisions and your sense of place. Consider how it can affect others.

*Great hope has no real footing unless one is willing to face into the doom that may also be on the way. . .*Norman Mailer

The older I get, the better I was.

What I don't like most about getting old is being unreliable.

My son put Christmas lights up over my nursing home bed. I can't do much these days, but I can do this: When someone enters, I turn on the twinkles. The staff sends people into my room so I can surprise them.

I realized it was me who was suffering over my mother's Alzheimer's when a caretaker explained, "She is living perfectly in the moment, like a butterfly." The prospect of me having this disease someday was suddenly less daunting.

I don't deal with the futility of figuring out why things happen. I embrace the intrigue of serendipity instead.

When I go to lunch, I leave a note on my nursing home bed that I've moved to Colorado. The staff named the lunchroom Colorado—my legacy.

If I lose my mind, I hope my family doesn't make personal sacrifices to accommodate my fate. If they feel guilty about that, I will be realizing my worst nightmare. So I remind them it is my deal, not theirs.

When I picked Dad up for church, I pointed out that his socks didn't match, he said, "That's how I roll."

I knew it was time to go into a home when my hearing got so bad I began watching old Lawrence Welk reruns on mute.

I've heard people say, "I changed my children's diapers. They can take care of me when I'm old." After all the sacrifices I've made for my children over the years, I'm certainly not going to lay that millstone on them and undo all the good I did.

When people give me rides, I leave strange things in their car like catalogues of tattoos or flyers on rattlesnake festivals or biker rallies.

Coloring with my grandchildren reintroduced me to the joy of that. I told my daughter, when I'm in a nursing home, bring me coloring books and crayons.

I told my children, "When I can't take care of myself anymore, you are to put me in a nursing home and don't you be coming down there and bothering me."

———————————

1. **When do you give up the car keys or your home?**

2. **How do you reconcile accepting reality with hoping for a miracle?**

3. **How do you gracefully accept the support of others while not burdening them? Do you hurt others when you refuse to share your difficulties with them?**

4. **What risks are associated with refusing to use canes, walkers, and wheelchairs?**

5. **How do you avoid excessive medical treatments?**

6. **How does planning influence transitions? Are long-term care insurance, health care directives, and legal documents helpful?**

CLOSING REMARKS:

There are many activities that don't require mental or physical agility. In the younger years of working and childrearing, there was little time for them—things like crossword and jigsaw puzzles, listening to music, playing cards and games, and reading books. When you are mashing pills in applesauce, dressing like a medieval peasant, and swimming becomes an activity equivalent to water boarding, you can do those things you didn't have time for before. You might be surprised by all the interesting things you can do. When something is lost, something else is gained.

When visiting a nursing home years ago, before they had alarms on the doors, I helped an elderly man in a wheelchair struggling to get inside. When I left, I helped him out. Sitting in my car, I observed him being helped in again only to reappear shortly thereafter with someone helping him out.

At first blush it appeared he had lost his mind, that he really wanted in and then really wanted out. However, he demonstrated considerable enthusiasm for the in-and-out process. I concluded he was conning people and enjoying the heck out of it.

This taught me not to underestimate nursing home residents. Odds are they are grifters who cheat at Bingo.

There are freedoms to be had in the latter phase of life. You can exercise your right to not take pills. You can refuse a colonoscopy, a mammogram, joint replacement, and a perm. You can eat all the butter, bacon, and ice cream you want. You can sell your car and put that money to better use. And you know for certain you will not die dusting, mowing a lawn, or trying not to swear during a plumbing project. People will cook for you. However your life plays out, at this point, your only job is to do aging well—or *beyond* well. To do that, a mantra is helpful.

A three-year-old hovered anxiously as his grandma, who considered a seat belt a complicated mechanical device, attempted to assemble a complex toy. Desperate to encourage Grandma's success, he reintroduced a phrase he used earlier the same day as she searched the kitchen for sprinkles for cookies, "YOU can do it." The little fellow's emphasis on the *you* was motivating, and Grandma became determined not to disappoint.

Since then, when aging issues made her feel as though she were being pushed onto a subway track, she thought about that desperate, hopeful little fellow's powerful words expressed in a squeaky little voice. "YOU can do it." And that became her mantra.

A mantra in your arsenal of coping tactics postures you to endure hardships. "YOU can do it," "Stay the course," "Work the problem," "Ride it down," "Buck up," or whatever other words of determination you come up with are motivating.

In addition to adopting your own coping strategies, helping others deal with your life experiences is a way to bless them. Loved ones tend to feel guilty if they don't try everything possible to save you from the consequences of aging, no matter the prospects. This can lead to bad decisions.

Just as people purchase an expensive casket they cannot afford for fear of not adequately honoring a loved one, they will approve futile and often invasive, painful, and expensive medical treatments to avoid the guilt of giving up on someone they love. You can prevent them from being swept down an irrational path by planning for contingencies, encouraging sensible, well-thought-out decisions, and insisting on rational treatment options. You can save them from the torturous scenario of observing you suffer excessive treatments by assuring that common sense prevails.

Anticipating prospects and planning for them means exploring appropriate legal documents and health care directives as well as long-term care and health insurance options. Consult experts, and communicate plans to those with an interest in your wellbeing. When they understand your intentions and are not surprised when the time comes to apply them, you soften their worlds.

When it comes to the inevitable *anti-bucket-list* experiences you are likely to face, know that "YOU can do it." Confront your issues with determination, courage, and even bravado. Do that for the people you care about. And remember, as long as you have someone to bring you ice cream, it is all good.

Let go gracefully of that which is no longer yours.

Chapter 16

A GOOD GOODBYE

*I've got this. I can do
this final act really well.*

**One of the most meaningful acts you will
perform in your lifetime is to show how to die.
Fate is unpredictable, but dying often presents an
opportunity to express love and to show how to
turn this final act into a blessing. How you choose
to experience dying has long-running implications.**
If fate dictates you cannot control the process
of dying, planning for it can do the job for you.
Preparing for the inevitable demonstrates how much
you care. People not brave enough to face the reality
of mortality often leave a mess for those they are
supposed to care about. This is a hurtful circumstance
to inflict on others when they are most vulnerable. It
generates anger and distracts from positive memories.

Contrast that with bucking up and giving the gift of a good goodbye. That is dying *beyond* well.

In our culture, death is viewed as an option. In the face of the inevitable, hopeless hope and denial reign. Cures are sought, unnecessary procedures performed, miracles solicited, and estates desecrated while reality is ignored. Hospice is helpful when a terminal illness is diagnosed. Unfortunately, it is often not sought until a couple of weeks before death.

Everyone is terminal. It is appropriate to fight the good fight when the prognosis supports it, but where fate dictates the end, ignoring that truth has a price. Denying impending death creates a void that can never be undone and a good goodbye unfulfilled. Conversely, facing death head on with courage and reason reveals the wonders of the cycle of life.

As much as you might prefer to avoid destiny, death will hit you hard with the loss of a loved one or your own doctor's report. You may be sitting cross-legged on an examining table with a gown tucked tightly under your butt and a physician says, "Go home and get your affairs in order."

It's tough to accept reality when it is revealed that a condition has become "the thing" that is going to get you. The inescapable truth is in your face: *You are only as strong as your weakest part.* Priorities change. Many matters in your life suddenly fade into the realm of insignificance. Others rise to the surface. Decisions must be made.

Hopeless hoping when death is unavoidable is often the source of savage consequences. Excessive end-of-life treatments are rampant in this country. A plethora of medical options, many that attack the sanctity of a patient's dignity, are offered up. This cannot be blamed entirely on the medical community.

A collaboration of doctor, patient, and family members is required to make this happen. Greed, medical philosophy, a for-profit medical system, complicated legal implications, and caring people clinging desperately to loved ones all converge to incentivize futile end-of-life treatments.

Elder abuse through medically unnecessary treatments promotes regrets, horrific memories, lingering hurt, plundered estates, and excessive legal fees. Family squabbles and lost opportunities to do dying well also result.

Conversely, unless death is sudden or mental capacity is lost, the opportunity exists to execute this final act with dignity and aplomb. Doing so offers the generous gift of a *good goodbye* to those you love. That influences how they grieve and whether they achieve peace with the loss. It also sets the stage for their own end-of-life experiences.

When you reach a level of serenity about your pending demise, you can engineer the process and enhance the ability of those you leave behind to move on. This influences how they perceive their own end-of-life process. This means how you handle this final act creates legacy. How important is that?

Fear keeps people from facing the harsh reality of dying. Fear inhibits planning for it. Fear prohibits a person from making their last experience a gift. Fear denies the cycle of life. To do dying *beyond* well, you must be brave, push past fear, go into the belly of the beast, and face that fear head on.

A woman was in her final days. Relatives and friends rallied around, but no one acknowledged the reality of her imminent demise. Living a lie, they tiptoed around reality like nothing important was happening. Bizarre conversations occurred about including her in future activities. "Grandma, when you get better I'll take you for a ride in my new truck." All this meant there would be no good goodbyes.

Because the dying experience was not being shared, futile and expensive medical procedures caused pain and turmoil while depleting the lady's estate.

When hospice became involved, rational thought prevailed. The family was persuaded to confront reality—to talk about what was happening. As a result, futile medical treatments were abandoned and palliative care introduced. Rich conversations flourished, "Grandma, what was the most important day in your life?"

The woman got her affairs in order. Rational decision-making prevailed. She reconciled with an estranged son, something that would not have happened otherwise. This was a gift to him, her, and others. The family was whole again.

Many other blessings ensued. The woman shared letters, photo albums, and memorabilia with her family. She told children and grandchildren stories they had never heard about their parents and ancestors. She gave precious items away, even gifting her wedding ring to her only granddaughter. Everyone got to say goodbye, and it was a good goodbye.

Planning is key to accomplishing a good goodbye. How do you plan when there are so many unknowns? Consider a line in the movie *The Big Chill,* "You can do what you can do." What you can do is own the experience, understand your options, take care of business, and simplify your life. Consult professionals and execute health care instructions (a living will), powers of attorney (for both financial and medical situations), a will, and in some cases, a trust. It is selfish not to get your affairs in order now while you can do so.

Understand the role hospice plays in end-of-life care so it is introduced in time to make a real difference. Typically, it is interjected so late in the process of dying that benefits are not optimized.

A way to help people through the grief they will experience when you are gone is to write poems or letters to be opened after your death. These are called *legacy letters*. Rich with encouraging words, they lift the burdens of others while also easing ones own. Such communications also provide an opportunity to show people that they matter—an extraordinary final gift.

The inevitable end of life—and the fact that, as an older person, you are so close to it and powerless to wholly orchestrate it—produces feelings that are fear-based and hugely disconcerting. When scary thoughts snake through your mind, remember this: *One of the most important things you will ever do is show how to die.*

There is an old Greek saying: "Old men plant trees whose shade they know they will never sit in." Have a plan for aging. Share your life story. Simplify your life. Be generous with your wisdom and possessions. Grant a good goodbye. Do these things for others—for their peace of mind and their future. Plant trees

---

*What happens after you die? They give someone else your hospital bed. . .*Jennifer Lawrence

I'm a pragmatic realist. There's no denial here. Someday my son will drop by for a visit and I'll say, "Well, I'm dying. Let's go on a cruise."

Die like a hero going home. . .Chief Tecumseh

I wonder if I died, how much the manager of Village Inn would miss me.

I've made peace with death. I just want someone to walk me home.

The final instruction in my mother's funeral plan was: "You kids take care of each other." That powerful directive, her ultimate wish, is hard to ignore. I included it in my funeral plan.

A man's dying mother asked him, "What do you think happens after death?" He said, "I don't know, Mom, but however it is, that's how it's supposed to be."

My goal in dying is to "leave it better."

I never understood why people make loved ones wait till they die to inherit their wealth? People waiting for me to die creeps me out. I'm giving my assets away now so I can watch those I care about enjoy them.

You might think you would not burden your children with an unfortunate ending, but ravages of the body and brain cannot be predicted. Plan for the end.

*. . .if the events of the last few years have taught me anything, it's that I'm going to feel like an idiot if I die tomorrow and I skimped on the bath oil today. So I use quite a lot of bath oil. . .*Nora Ephron

———————————

1. How do you know when to give up on life and accept the inevitable? How do you convince others to accept that reality?

2. If someone proposes futile, expensive, and painful medical treatments during the end-of-life stage, how do you avoid that?

3. How do you become educated on hospice's services? How do you include that in end-of-life planning? How do you convince loved ones to seek hospice services?

4. How does planning for end-of-life scenarios soften the blow of them for you and others?

5. Have you considered gifting possessions while you are still here so you can share in the joy of the receivers rather than them inheriting things when you are gone?

6. How important is funeral planning? How can you make your funeral meaningful?

7. How important are legacy letters? What would

you write if you knew you were going to die?

8. What else can you do to "plant trees"?

CLOSING COMMENTS:

A boy being tucked into bed the night before his birthday said, "Goodbye five. I'll never see you again." Someday, you may have the opportunity to deliver a poignant goodbye. Make it a good one.

Legacy letters are powerful. They have the potential to create stunning outcomes. When well executed, such letters lift burdens, heal wounds, and spark dreams. It is possible your death can be someone else's beginning.

You can leave legacy letters for people to read after you are gone or give them to people in your final days and witness their responses.

Don't wait until you know you are dying to write legacy letters. Do it now. This is the story of a woman who wished she had such a treasure:

> In the last year of her life, Mother transitioned into an unhappy soul. I wanted to save her, but could not. I loved her so, and tried desperately to find a warm connection again, but most contact was difficult and draining. I know intellectually she couldn't help it. Still,

the end hurt. In a sense, I lost my mother long before she died. I didn't experience a good goodbye.

Focusing on memories of earlier years and the awesome mother she was gives me comfort, but it is impossible to erase how she was at the end. The emotional abandonment of a parent during the final stage of their life is tough. It's a burden I carry, but it is also life happening. I imagine how I might have felt if I had a letter she had written before she got so bad. Lesson learned. I will write some letters.

Here are ideas on what to write about in *legacy letters* to loved ones.

I want to thank you for. . .
My favorite memory of you is. . .
I want to apologize to you for. . .
I understand, and I forgive you for. . .
I want you to know. . .
The fabulous qualities about you are. . .
I enjoyed watching you. . .
I wish for you that. . .

Make your letters inspirational—something that will improve a person's life going forward. Make them intimate, personal communications so rich, wonderful, and significant that they are passed down through generations.

Plan for your demise. Don't put it off. A lack of planning creates anger and frustration for those left behind. If you have no will or have not shared it with your beneficiaries, odds are your worst nightmare will materialize—your family fighting over your estate. Take the appropriate legal steps, and share your plan. (Most arguments over estates occur because someone is surprised by the will or funeral plan.) Show love by smoothing processes for others.

Plan your funeral. Death can come so suddenly that it is as though it were a mistake. The shock of it exacerbates poor decision-making. It is not unusual for survivors to make unfortunate, costly choices at such times. Planning helps prevent this.

Be cautious about including instructions in your plan that are difficult to carry out. They can create lingering guilt when others want to do what you requested but cannot pull it off. Designating someone to speak at your funeral who is not emotionally equipped to do so creates pressure. A song you request might not work well for the person you expect to sing it. Instructions may make others uncomfortable for some reason you are not aware of, or they may be impractical to carry out.

A man wanted a motion detector device in his tombstone that set off a recording in his voice that said, "Get off of me." This was a quirky, humorous idea that entertained survivors, but it was impractical to implement.

Another man wanted his ashes spread on top of a specific mountain. This was a problem for his loved ones, none of whom were mountain climbers.

Such situations can be avoided with a statement in the plan that it's okay to not follow any instructions that prove difficult to carry out. Words such as *if, perhaps, maybe, may, might, unless,* and *whatever* in the instructions imply permission for those executing the plan to do what works for them. Such flexibility facilitates the funeral preparation process and softens the world of those struggling with loss.

You might suggest epitaph options. A man playfully suggested these: "I told you I was sick." "It seemed important at the time." "I couldn't stop picking at it." Survivors may suspect you were out on a day pass when you came up with epitaph alternatives, but by setting a fun tone, you take the edge off the process. Aside from silly options, your suggestion of a serious one can relieve survivors of the burden of creating one. Writing your own obituary can have a similar result. Invite survivors to revise your epitaph and obituary as they see fit.

You have probably been to funerals so generic that they could have been for anyone. And there are those where the program is so contrary to the nature of the person who died that the service is downright disrespectful. An attempt to save souls at the funeral of an agnostic is inappropriate. This usually happens because there is no funeral plan. In contrast, services that articulate the essence of the person being eulogized are the result of planning. These services are lush with personal reflections and messages to live by. Here is an example of one:

> The man doing the eulogy said, "If you had Ron for a friend, you didn't need any other friends. Ron saw past people's flaws and discovered what made them special. Anytime a friend was in trouble, he was the *go to* guy.
>
> "As a couple of friends were driving home after late night partying, they observed Ron headed downtown. One joked to the other, 'Ron must be on his way to bail someone out of jail.' The next day, they learned that is exactly what he did. Friends could count on Ron. He believed in second chances. He invested in people."
>
> The speaker pointed his finger at the audience and swept it from one side of the room to the other and back again as he said, "Ron Mainer may not have bailed you out of jail, but he invested in each and every one of you here. *You owe him a return on his investment.*"

That comment articulated Ron's legacy. If you want to live with passion and purpose, invest in people. If you want to experience bliss, invest in people. If you want to leave it better, invest in people. If you want to invest in people, do dying well. The return will be your reward—your legacy.

A little girl had an enthusiastic older brother whom she idolized. He was fascinated with super powers. She told her mother, "I want to be a super power, too." Unable to imagine her daughter in a Spiderman costume, Mom asked, "What kind of super power?" The girl pondered that a moment and then replied, "A strong butterfly." Mom made a costume and the girl adopted that persona. Over time, the concept of a strong butterfly described her perfectly as she evolved into a beautiful, colorful, self-assured, little go-getter.

Words are powerful. Identify words that define you. Share them in expressions to others, and include them in end-of-life planning. And when it is your time, bring it. Be a strong butterfly or whatever other personification you choose to describe your super power. Take that power, and go for a good goodbye.

Peace is found through acceptance of the inevitable.

BEYOND AGING WELL **EXAMPLES**

Example: Legacy Letters In Poetry Form

If I Could Miss

If I could miss when life is over. . .

My son, I would miss your risky thrills
that stir my world and give me chills.
I would miss your nurturing heart,
your fortitude, and knack for art.

My daughter, I would miss your loving heart
that speaks to all and joy imparts.
I would miss your strong devotion,
resourcefulness, and deep emotion.

My son, I would miss your guitar singing
and all the music it is bringing.
I would miss your clever wit,
your gentle ways, and strong spirit.

And babies all, so small and sweet,
twinkling stars I'm blessed to meet,
I would miss your innocence
and all the exploits you do since.

To all of you, I bequeath
the legacy I aim to teach.
I always knew and understood
each of you were marked for good.

You kids take care of each other.

You Matter
Just by *Being*, You Are Enough

There is a place inside of you.
It is strong and you are, too.
It is yours and yours alone,
the essence only you can own.

No one can break it.
No one can take it.
You hurt and it will pull you through.
Always, always it will save you.

Keep the Faith - Stay the Course

When times are hard, remember this:

"You are braver than you believe,
stronger than you seem, and
smarter than you think."—Christopher Robin

Example: Poem On Aging

Vintage with Game—or Not

I am a woman laced with contradictions—dancing duets
of oppositions.

I am old. Seventy is old by any definition.
Aging is embraced, for it is a gift.
Inebriated with gratefulness, I relish every day.
Still, reality is a severe and angry truth—tsunamis threaten.
The gradual decline haunts. Suddenly-one-moment
    incidents hover like angry poltergeists.
Not ready, it is as though aging is happening to someone else.
And I am just a voyeur.

I am relevant. I make a difference.
Enlightenment is sought through continuous learning.
I generously share knowledge and resources.
Opportunities to coast are resisted and purpose—
    a focus on creating legacy—prevails.
The intention is to matter—and I do.
Still, my youth is mourned.
For in the eyes of the young, I have begun to disappear.

I am aging beyond well. This is my time.
These are encore years—better than the original show.
I celebrate life by cherishing wisdom acquired and by
    reveling in the fruits of my work.
In the mirror, a magnificent being is reflected.
I admire the resilience etched in the deeply-inhabited face.
On another day, though, I recoil from the same image.
Jolted by this revelation, I wonder if I am bipolar.

I have a zest for life, which is on full display.
Reveling in the tenuous now, I ignore the precarious future.
A pervasive uneasiness smolders, though.
Ghost-like, it torments with the terror of something grave.
I dream of it—a cloud that nudges me awake at night.
As coffee soothes, a gnawing anxiety remains.
There will be no more sleep this night, for I fear I cannot
      save myself.

I am strong—at least somewhat and sometimes.
Ignoring frailties, I go all out—until fate prevails.
Then, I pretend vigor. In private, I melt into feebleness.
Harsh truths reveal I am only as strong as my weakest part.
Physical vulnerabilities gnaw at my gut.
Prospects torture for I know I am a ticking time bomb.
I shake like a baby rabbit in a human hand because
      to the universe I am prey.

I am smart—smart enough.
Overachievement proffers intelligence, and I do amazing
      things through shear determination.
The brain has gotten lazy, though, and stupid things happen.
In the shower, I discover on my face the reading glasses
      I searched for all morning.
I find another pair on my head.
The people hiding in my attic steal the remote.
And I don't know the difference between HD and analog.

I am philosophical.
No one has all the answers, myself included,
But I am well-seasoned, and introspection blossoms.
Accepting apologies I never got, I grant forgiveness.
I don't believe things happen for a reason, but I know
      everything matters and everyone matters.
When I feel regret, though, salvation is found in concluding
      most blunders don't matter.
Resigned and resilient, I press on.

I am steady and responsible.
However, the depth of my strength is shallow, and I am
    stingy with commitments.
Duty be damned, my rejuvenation takes precedence.
Rules are broken, and obligations shirked.
Audacious and brave, selfish and miserly, I don't step up.
There are no regrets—or so I pretend.
Contrition haunts, and covertly I lament my derelictions.

I am proper.
I aspire to an appropriate level of dignity.
But nice is boring and the refined tedious.
So I do things I shouldn't—irreverent, inappropriate,
    bat-shit-crazy things.
Like a third-base coach waving a runner home, I encourage
    others to do the same.
My child hears of these escapades and threatens:
"Don't make me come over there."

Realistic and pragmatic—I am often the voice of reason.
I am also increasingly impulsive—reckless even.
I no longer edit my words or actions as others require.
Spirited friends egg me on for we have nothing to lose.
We are barred from a coffee shop for noise and from a
    sushi bar for a food fight.
The young are astounded we have more fun than they do.
My child asks, "And how old are you people?"

I relish the fellows.
But I am no longer the woman who notices a man and
    sucks in her stomach and stands up straighter.
Love is a powerful temptress that cannot be trusted.
Hugs are harvested, which comfort but do not complete.
Prospects are murdered lest something inside of me breaks again.
Though yearning persists, I don't have another breakup in me.
A void intrudes, which I fill with chocolate.

I am beautiful. If I live long enough, I'll be cute again.
Visible deterioration is interpreted as patina—a lovely tarnish.
But it is not lovely, so the sad, sorry truth is ignored—buried.
I stare at the naked waffle woman in the mirror and
     fantasize I look better from the back. But I don't.
On a sidewalk, a vaguely familiar reflection appears in a window.
I wonder, "Who is that old woman?"
Age bitch slaps me—hard—as reality storms in. It is me.

I am all these things—a mighty woman.
Colliding with the stereotype, I rage, reframe, transform,
     and evolve.
I say to people, "*This* is what seventy looks like."
I resolve that this is my time—my best time—and it is.
I'm *vintage with game*. Yeah, that's it. I've got game.
Naaah, I don't. Not really.
Yes, I do. I do. I really do. No, I don't. Yes. No. Yes?

Although age is a persistent intruder, I soldier on—a
woman laced with contradictions.

Example: Fictional Short Story
(Express unrealized dreams by writing about them.)

Sometimes Mavis
Does Things She Shouldn't

Mavis squirms in the seat of her Lexus as she observes traffic backing up. The street light, disabled by a passing thunderstorm, flashes red. Every driver must stop and maneuver through a helter-skelter mess of vehicles.

A police car moseys through the intersection. Because of its leisurely pace, Mavis concludes the policemen inside have nothing better to do than to direct traffic. She is irritated that they do not do so. She always wanted to direct traffic.

Mavis is a *can do* gal. Before retirement, she ran a company where she didn't tolerate inaction when bad things happened to customers or employees. She told her staff, "Do something—even if it's wrong." She wanted to put *dammit* on the end of that sentence but, of course, she couldn't do that. Corporate America frowns on such language. In her mind, those policemen have an obligation to "do something" about the traffic backup. *Dammit.*

Now retired, Mavis enjoys not having to comply with workplace restrictions or to worry about her reputation. As a result, she's become a bit of a pistol. She often does things she shouldn't these days.

When she and her friends got into a food fight in a sushi bar, her children chastise her with "Don't make me come over there," a threat she often made to them when they were children.

Mavis eases her way up to the light as traffic allows while becoming more and more impatient. Although she has all day, she knows other people have someplace to be. So when she spots a driveway just short of the intersection, she pulls in, parks, gets out, and proceeds to the middle of the intersection.

Surely a strange sight—a frail old lady in yoga wear with hair looking like a tangle of fishing lures—Mavis begins directing traffic. Awkward at first, she soon masters the flow of the process and orders cars this way and that with abandon. The rhythm of the movements reminds her of disco dancing back in 1978. Drivers wave in appreciation. Some honk. Most are laughing.

A police car pulls up. Two cops approach. They try to appear official, although the look of amusement on their faces belies their attempt at an authoritative demeanor.

"Ma'am, you can't do this."

"Why not?"

"It's against the law."

"Well, you do it then."

Mavis considers tacking *dammit* on the end of her proposal. She doesn't only out of respect for law enforcement and because one of the officers reminds her of her grandson. She ignores them and continues exuberantly waving cars through the intersection, her moves now crisp yet fluid. She resists the temptation to spin, but allows a bit of hip movement to invade the process. She wishes she had a whistle.

Drivers take note of the confrontation, and honking escalates. A teenager hanging out of a passenger window bangs his hand against the side of the car and yells, "Take 'em out, Grandma."

The policemen shift their weight from foot to foot. They do not want to arrest this old woman, but their mission requires that they protect her from herself. They move in closer.

Refusing to be distracted from the task at hand, Mavis keeps her eyes on the traffic.

"You're not going to tase me, are you?" she asks as her arm swirls in broad circles, skillfully guiding drivers on their way in an orderly manner.

"No, we wouldn't do that."

Both the officers and Mavis know that would not be necessary. They could easily lift her tiny frame by the arms and carry her off with her feet circling as though she were riding a bicycle. They are prepared to do so. Mavis senses this, stares belligerently at them for a moment, then turns and stomps toward her car, arms swinging, shoulders hunched, her head leading her body. Drivers honk like crazy. The officers are relieved. The drivers are irritated. Some yell out of their windows.

As Mavis settles into the hot leather seat of her car, she considers how things might have ended differently. A policeman could have said, "Have a seat. Watch your head." Or she could have been loaded into an ambulance with him asking, "Ma'am, can you describe the car that hit you? Ma'am? Ma'am?"

Although disappointed that her dissidence was cut short, Mavis smiles as she puts the key in the ignition. She always wanted to direct traffic, and she thinks about how sometimes she does things she shouldn't. As she pulls out of the parking lot, Mavis makes a mental note to pick up a whistle the next time she goes to the store.

(*Red Heels and Smokin' — How I Got My Moxie Back*)

Example: Memoir Turned Into Fiction

(A fiction piece loosely based on a group of
retired people who meet routinely at a local coffee shop.)

The Pillars of Sloth

Sporting a Grizzly Adams beard, khaki pants, and hiking boots, Tucker was the first *Pillar of Sloth* to arrive at The Crescent Coffee Shop. He scored a table for six. A brainy, retired college professor, Tucker is known as The Mountain Man because of his massive frame and love of Colorado. In spite of being highly educated and accomplished, his dignity is challenged by nasal incontinence, which means when he laughs, coffee comes out of his nose. Tucker is mutilated by a misspelled tattoo (a remnant of his military days), which says, "No Regerts."

Annie Ann, whose stunning silver hair drapes softy over her shoulders, showed up sporting a highly engineered cane capable of standing up by itself. Members of the group suspect it contains a taser. Annie Ann's sassy nature generally hides behind an overt sweet persona. When fired up, though, her cane and her words are lethal.

Olivia, a retired corporate executive and the group's voice of reason, joined the group. She suggested to Annie Ann that she sit in her chair *normal* because she fell out of it last time and flailed around on the floor like a turtle on its back until helpers got her up. Tucker, who has never given up on possessing a woman, offered to hold Annie Ann in place and slid his arm around her. She said, "In your wildest dreams," and stomped his foot hard with her cane. He reacted as though he'd been tased.

Wanda, an uninhibited rebel and the least proper of the group, arrived. She considers herself a fashionista. With orange bleached hair, tight jeans, and silver knee-high boots, à la Wonder Woman style, she was styling—sort of.

Wally, a slight, angular man, whose disposition leans toward the cantankerous, showed up. He can't hear so good but refuses to wear hearing aids. This means he lives in a world of *What just happened?* His primary contribution to conversation is "WHAT?"

Godfrey, a retired technical wizard and sci-fi devotee, shuffled in. He usually arrives late and moves at the pace of a glacier, so the group hums the Alfred Hitchcock Show theme song when he enters. It perfectly matches his lumbering pace. He often wears a broad-brimmed hat, which he believes helps people remember him, but mostly they just remember the hat. It comes in handy at coffee because Wanda throws food at him. Because of this ongoing feud, he carries an umbrella no matter the weather.

As the guys settled in, Tucker reported he had a leaky carburetor. He wasn't talking about his car.

Godfrey gave a report on his thyroid.

Wanda, not accustomed to editing her remarks, reported that she had no thyroid—or ovaries.

Wally missed most of the conversation but picked up on the word "ovaries" and said, "WHAT?"

To steer the discussion away from medical issues, Olivia said, "Speaking of sex." This was meant as a distraction, not an invitation to talk about the subject. Nevertheless, Wally picked up on *sex* and said, "WHAT?" Tucker, taking Olivia's suggestion literally, told a joke about an old couple who had sex every Sunday to the pace of church bells ringing. The old fellow died one morning when an ice cream truck went by. This caused Tucker's nasal incontinence to kick in as everyone laughed except Wally, who wondered *What just happened?*

Hoping to be on topic, although he had no clue what the topic was, Wally reported, "I watched Harrison Ford pierce Jimmy Fallon's ear on television last night." The group suggested he rethink his DVR selections. He said, "WHAT?" Annie Ann asked, "What is a DVR?"

Wanda said, "Judge Judy told some guy he wouldn't be any stupider if someone cut his head off —or was that Dr. Phil, or Maury?" Godfrey suggested she rethink her DVR selections and gave an update on the reality show *Finding Sasquatch*, which he believed meant scientists were on the verge of a watershed scientific breakthrough.

Honoring their ongoing feud, Wanda threw a pecan at Godfrey. It landed on his hat. Knowing there would be another, he ignored it.

Wanda, the only one of the group getting any dating action, updated the group on her experience with a Vietnam vet who had convinced her weed was a condiment. "He has some powerful stuff that makes my teeth feel big." The group stared at her mystified

—not so much about the weed, but the teeth thing. She gazed wistfully at her coffee cup for a moment and then revealed she missed her ex-husband, a fireman who ran off with a waitress who got her toe stuck in a bathtub faucet. She said, "My ex is a consummate rescuer." No one argued that point.

Olivia advised the group that gospel singers on The Lawrence Welk Show once sang *One Toke Over the Line, Sweet Jesus* on television. The group debated whether Welk or the singers knew what the song was about. Wanda Googled the show on her smart phone and passed it around. When it got to Godfrey, he held up his end of the feud and hid it in the belt line of his pants.

A sweet potato nugget whizzed by Godfrey's head, smacked against the wall, and fell to the floor. No one reacted because the incident was not that unusual— a Wanda payback—which suggested why the group was kicked out of The Mulberry Street Coffee Shop.

Wanda reported she and her Vietnam vet boyfriend ate the best raisins in the universe and a whole box of Lucky Charms after their movie date Saturday night.

Mountain Man Tucker, dabbed a napkin on the coffee dripping from his nose and recounted a story about a man with a wooden leg being eaten alive by termites. He had reported this matter on previous occasions. Picking up on the group's lack of interest, he turned his attention to his empty plate, which a few minutes ago held a cinnamon roll the size of a small dog. He stared at the plate intently for a moment and then said, "My doctor warned me that if I keep eating sugar, I'll end up in a diabetic coma."

This inspired several other "my doctor told me" stories from the group followed by Godfrey giving a report on his colonoscopy. Knowing that everyone in the group had had a colonoscopy, Olivia said, "Speaking of sex."

The group spoke about sex. People at the next table eavesdropped. People at the next table left. People at another nearby table left.

Wanda's phone vibrated and slipped out of the belt line of Godfrey's pants. As he stood up to retrieve it, Wanda offered to help, which caused the two to circle the table twice. Godfrey shook his right leg intermittently until the phone fell out onto the floor. Tucker grabbed it and put it in his pocket. Wanda tried to retrieve it, and another pursuit ensued. Embarrassed by this behavior, Olivia suggested the group contemplate the world situation.

Wanda interrupted with a report on the Red Dot Shoe Sale at Macy's and speculated on whether it included boots.

Wally passed an amazing fart for such a small man. Godfrey announced, "Someone stepped on a duck," and everyone scattered for coffee refills. Wally couldn't hear the duck and initially wondered, *What just happened?* Then he figured it out.

Wanda's phone ringtone was a quacking duck, and it began quacking in Tucker's pocket as he refilled his coffee cup at the self-service table. This caused him to slosh coffee down the front of his khaki Mountain Man pants. Several women offered to help dry him off. Annie Ann prevailed since she carried a small, battery-powered fan in her purse. The drying activity caught the attention of several patrons and the coffeeshop's service staff.

As the air cleared and the gang regrouped, Godfrey noticed Wanda sprinkling raisins on an ample supply of yogurt and opened his umbrella.

After further discussions of online crazy cat videos and whether "the blues" could be played on a ukulele, Wally was the first to leave. Someone told him to have a nice day. He said, "WHAT?" So the goodwill message was repeated in unison by all members of the group, "HAVE A NICE DAY." He responded, "I've got other plans." Annie Ann also left after successfully sitting in her chair *normal*.

Wanda said "Chow" and headed out to Macy's. Godfrey closed his umbrella while announcing that the psycho thriller he was reading was so full of flourish that it represented literary masturbation. Olivia responded with a comment of literary substance when Tucker interrupted with a thought that excited him. "Oh, oh, oh! Grey Goose is gluten free and contains no sugar."

Olivia, always the voice of reason, wrestled with her coat as she gave her usual response to nonsensical remarks. "We are all still *Pillars of Sloth*, though, aren't we?" Tucker nodded and took a swig of coffee. He sat there alone, staring at his empty plate and contemplating the prospect of his doctor cutting off his toes and the challenges of tattoo removal.

(Red Heels and Smokin' - How I Got My Moxie Back)

Example: Memoir In Short Story Form

Being Thelma and Louise

Mom was seventy-five and I fifty-four when we became *Thelma and Louise.* I'd say, "Get in the car, Thelma." Her eyes would light up like a child discovering a fluffy puppy. Always up for an adventure, she grabbed her purse and cane and shuffled to the garage at an amazing pace given her bad hips and knees.

Before Dad died, he often surprised Mom with spontaneous escapades. When he said, "Get in the car, Mom," she was ready. They set off for destinations to which she was not privy until they got there. I suspect my invitations reminded her of those impromptu adventures, and that she delighted in the feelings our trips resurrected.

Mom never saw the *Thelma and Louise* movie, so she wasn't sure what to think when I assigned us that label. She seemed up for it, though. There was no protest when I announced that I got to be Louise, the character who shot somebody—not that Mom would have wanted that role anyway. An Iowa farm woman immersed in heartland conformity, she was not inclined to aspire to criminal activity.

After Dad died, I brought her from rural Iowa to Tulsa, Oklahoma, for long visits to distract from the grief that threatened to overwhelm her. She was in a vulnerable state. In addition to the loss of Dad, declining physical abilities were taking hold. The responsibility of caring for her weighed on me. I worried she would fall. She had a small dog who was on his last leg. He accompanied her on those visits. I was concerned he would die on my watch and generate even more grief. I also agonized over the prospect that Mom would trip over him, fall on him, hurt herself, and kill the dog.

Since I worked, Mom sat alone all day surveilling the neighborhood activity through my townhouse window while occupying herself with jigsaw puzzles, word games, and crochet. Out of her element in my downtown Tulsa townhouse, she expressed considerable curiosity about the destinations of passing cars. In her rural environment, she could predict where neighbors were headed by the direction they were going, the day of the week, and the time of day. The anonymity of my neighbors and my lack of interest in their business baffled her.

Feeling guilty about leaving her alone all day, I planned adventures for the evenings. We patronized our favorite restaurants. Extensive menus and generous portions disturbed her. She would say, "I'll just eat off your plate," which irritated me. Her extreme frugality prompted her to stuff table items and condiments into her purse, in which she carried plastic bags for table scraps and a knife with which to cut them up.

After dinner, we hit craft stores and specialty shops. I held her hand from the car to shopping carts, carefully navigating curbs, sidewalk flaws, and door jams. The tender nature of this action comforted me.

Her hands were soft, her fingers long and slender, her grasp gentle but sure. We fit together with a naturalness possible only through common ancestry. I have her hands. My daughter does as well. I look at my granddaughter's tiny hands and wonder. . .

We developed an easy banter, and she took on the mission of getting the better of me. This drew out the smart aleck in me, which she pretended to find disgusting but secretly enjoyed. The twinkle in her eyes betrayed her.

Detailers left the moonroof cover open on my car. I pushed every button in that vehicle trying to close it, creating a host of other problems. This included interior lights permanently lit, which had me driving around town looking like an all-night casino. I complained about the predicament to Mom as we took off on a road trip. She reached up, slid the moonroof cover shut, and sat there smiling like a Cheshire cat who had left a fur ball on my spot on the sofa. I decided to take advantage of her mechanical aptitude. I asked, "Why don't you shut off the interior lights, smart ass?" And she did.

Although we were girlfriends at this point, she never completely abandoned her maternal role. I often read into the night, which in her mind was wrong. She showed up in my bedroom doorway late one night in a floral patterned nightgown representative of wallpaper. Wild-eyed and wobbly, everything about her seemed askew. Her hair resembled a fright wig that had been attacked by a feline. Waving her cane, she was a scary sight.

"You're going to go blind," she scolded in a raspy voice.

A patronizing lecture ensued against which I held my position, "You are not the boss of me."

She eventually shuffled back to bed, mumbling something about a home for the blind and debtors' prison. As my heart rate gradually returned to normal, I resumed reading.

Such a conniption fit was rare. Mom was generally meek and mild mannered. On our road trips, it was not uncommon for me to be stopped by the highway patrol. Having spent considerable time on patrol with sheriff's deputies in the past, I viewed any opportunity to interact with law enforcement as an adventure extraordinaire. In contrast, Mom was traumatized the second the blue and red lights started flashing. She never did acclimate to the experience, and it was no comfort to her that we never got a ticket.

Mom was just the sidekick I needed to get out of one. I had developed a nifty, failsafe routine to do so. Here's how it worked:

Mom looked like Mrs. Santa Claus —short, round, white hair, and old-fashioned glasses. She sported a silver helmet-head, permed hairdo and wore calico print dresses. A purse usually hung from her arm à la Queen Elizabeth's style.

When pulled over, I would roll down the window, point to her, and tell the patrolman, "She made me do it."

When he leans down to take a look, he discovers Mom in the passenger seat frozen with fear. Her lack of eye contact is reminiscent of a dog who had peed on the living room rug. The only movement comes from the hands in her lap, wringing a handkerchief.

After allowing the patrolman time to take that in, I ask, "Would you take her to jail?"

If that doesn't get a laugh, I lean out the window and whisper, "You know, she kidnapped me."

When additional drama is required, I apply my *coup d'état* and tell him, "We are *Thelma and Louise*, and *she* is the one who shot somebody."

An Oklahoma patrolman called my bluff when I asked him to take Mom to jail. In a strong southern accent, he said, "I'd do that, ma'am, but I *would* have to tase her first." This produced an unpleasant visual in my mind, and I decided to skip the kidnapping routine and allow him the last word.

"Your passenger looks suspicious—a threat to any community," he said. "Git on down the road to Missouri and don't make any stops along the way."

We didn't get a ticket.

I took Mom everywhere, even out with my single friends. The guys asked her out on dates, and I threatened to shoot them. Married all her life, she was perplexed by my single lifestyle. Terrorizing her over my exploits became a temptation too enticing to resist.

Dressed in leather pants for a date, I asked her, "Am I sexy yet?"

I followed up with, "I wear leather on dates so I smell like a new truck."

Borrowing one of Dad's lines, she said, "You are one watt short of a nightlight."

In spite of that protestation, she must have thought I looked smart, because she took my picture. As I was leaving with my date, she said, "Don't call me if you get thrown in jail."

This was a familiar threat I had heard often during my teenage years. It was confounding to my date, though. His plans for the evening did not include getting arrested.

* * *

Thelma and I haunted a casino primarily for the buffet—or so we said. In Mom's mind, gambling was a sin. She made me promise not to reveal her vice to church friends in Iowa.

We were not sophisticated gamblers. The first time we hit the casino, we carried sandwich baggies of coins from my change jar. I had no idea slot machines had gone coinless. And I was shocked and disappointed to discover the levers had been replaced with buttons. Yes, buttons. A casino security officer observed us old ladies trying to locate an opening for coins in a nickel slot machine. He oriented us on the modern nuances of gambling. In return, we were rude and inconsiderate. "Shoot. I wanted to pull the handles," Mom complained while frantically pounding buttons and staring transfixed at spinning cherries.

"Me, too. This is a bummer," I said as I hammered away on my own buttons.

In ten minutes our money was gone, and we ambled over to the buffet.

* * *

I took Mom to the office with me one day where she chastised the president of the company for requiring me to drive across the state for business. She said, "You men should be doing that." After thirty years of striving for equal footing in corporate America, this was not the kind of help I needed. Fortunately, Mom was cute and most likely representative of the president's own mother. With a twinkle in his eye he promised to look into the prospect of grounding me. Mom left his office stepping high, proud that she had rescued me from the depths of corporate hell.

* * *

I took Mom on trips. A novice traveler, having rarely been out of Iowa, or even her own community, she had no concept of diversity. We ventured all the way to Hawaii where she worried about being a burden to me.

"If I get sick, throw me in the ocean," she said.

"I don't think my brothers would appreciate it if I took their mother on vacation and fed her to the sharks. I'll put you in a paraglider, though," I said.

"I don't know what that is, but the idea sounds like something your dad would come up with."

I suspected she had that thought often. Although my physical characteristics mimicked Mom's, my way of being in the world had Dad written all over it.

Soon after arriving in Hawaii, we sat at a sidewalk cafe sipping pineapple drinks with umbrellas in them. Mom suddenly froze and took on an expression of grave concern.

"Mom, what's wrong?"

Through squinted eyes and with furrowed brow, she looked both ways to make certain no one could hear her. Leaning over the table, she whispered, "All these people here are foreigners." The perplexed look on her face when I explained that, in Hawaii, *she* was the foreigner, reflected the depth of her naiveté.

Having rarely left Iowa, Mom had little sense of other people or places. When we visited Salt Lake City, she worried the mountains would slide in on us. In Dallas, the traffic had her in a state of awesome wonder. She expressed a burning desire to know where all those people were going. After spending years in a small trailer and apartment, she could not grasp why anyone would want to ramble around in such big houses.

In wonderful places, she said, "I don't know why anyone would want to live here." This observation came from a woman who lived a couple of miles from a pig farm in Iowa. When the wind blew in the right direction, the place smelled like. . .like. . .like a pig farm.

On a trip to California, I took her to Venice Beach, a place reminiscent of an extreme *Rocky Horror Picture Show* party.

I explained common beach apparel, "She's not naked as a jaybird, Mom. She's wearing a thong bikini."

I clarified beach activities, "No, Mom, body piercing is not a magic act."

I suggested brazen adventures. "Mom, let's get a tattoo. This skull and crossbones looks interesting. It's about pirates. We love pirates."

I don't believe Mom had ever seen a tattoo. She had a way of puffing her cheeks when something appalled her. Staring at the conspicuous tattoo of a lightening bolt shooting out of a young man's butt crack, she puffed like a blowfish. In her Christmas letter that year, she wrote, "There sure are a lot of weird people in California."

She squeezed my hand tight and grabbed my arm as a pack of roller skaters whizzed by, barely missing us, as we ambled along the beach sidewalk. The skates made a horrendous racket and their music blared the sort of sounds we old gals considered obnoxious nonsense.

"What the hell was that?" she asked.

Shocked, I responded, "Mom, you swore."

She covered her mouth and lowered her head in shame—mock shame, I suspected. Our adventures had inspired in her a newfound level of spunk. Reinforcing her moxie, I assured her that Thelma would, no doubt, have sworn in such a circumstance. In the past, the only time I ever heard her swear was when she fell on my front porch. I was so taken aback by her language that I failed to ask if she was hurt. Instead, I said, "Mom, you swore!"

As her health deteriorated, our excursions became limited to trips around her senior housing apartment in Iowa. We were still *Thelma and Louise,* but the days of big adventures were behind us. Festering health crises gained momentum. She went into a nursing home at eighty-eight, where she was chastised by church ladies for swearing during card games. She was also disciplined by staff for speeding in her wheelchair.

In the midst of a severe medical episode, she slipped off her wedding ring, handed it to me, and we cried. Mom rallied the next day, so I put it back on her finger after which I held on tight to that precious hand that nurtured me all my life. It was clear where she was headed.

She died a few months later. The times we shared were sweet. We were girlfriends—carousing, teasing, and giggling. We were tight. We were *Thelma and Louise,* although we never shot anybody. And we never got a ticket.

(*A River of Stories*, Tulsa NightWriters Anthology)

Example: Memoir In Art Form

A Life Quilt

A life quilt portrays a person's history in a quilt-like pattern on poster board, foam board, or some other surface. Inherent in the process of creating it is a *life review*. This activity requires interpreting the past from a fresh, mature perspective. The quilt visually expresses those interpretations.

This pseudo-quilt can be framed or placed under glass on a tabletop. It is perfect for displaying at birthday celebrations of the person portrayed.

A series of squares are outlined on poster board or whatever surface is selected. Each is decorated to symbolize a period of time in the person's life.

Scrapbooking sections in craft stores contain a plethora of creative tags, stickers, tape, fabric, and art supplies with which to depict a life. Colors and designs for each square reflect the activities and tone of that time. The last square is a representation of the future.

Good times and bad times may occupy the same amount of space but, depending on their intensity and significance, some colors and patterns are protruding while others are subtle. Because of space constraints, decisions must be made on what to include and what to leave out. What rises to the top is interesting and, in some cases, surprising.

THE CHILDHOOD YEARS are typically portrayed with primary colors and playful patterns, calico prints, and nuances of earlier times. However, for some people, these early years are clouded with muted colors, perhaps even black, and complicated patterns that reflect turmoil, anxiety, and danger.

TEEN YEARS often reflect hectic, intense designs with pop art qualities dressed up in bright colors—oranges, reds, and yellows.

CHILD REARING YEARS portrayed in shades of blue and pink demonstrate parental awakening and intense nurturing.

For many, THE THIRTIES are composed of cohesive, structured patterns with shades of green representing maturity, responsibility, and an absence of severe risk-taking.

In contrast, THE FORTIES might include sharp edges, bold patterns, and strong colors representing midlife turmoil and forced change. The interjection of dark colors reflects harsh traumas.

THE FIFTIES for some would consist of a flurry of purple and pear green or blues and yellows—complementary colors. They depict coming out of midlife turmoil and settling in, just before aging becomes an emerging issue.

THE SIXTIES decade for many people is rich with freedom and rebirth influences. Happy colors and sunburst patterns are appropriate. A dose of contrasting brown and black hues symbolizes the introduction of escalating losses and recognition of inevitable decline.

THE SEVENTIES invites patterns and colors emphasizing the wonders of this time. Bursts of soft apricots, lavenders and other pastels are interrupted with shades of gray. Muted hues symbolize acceptance and resignation. Black may be introduced depending on the level of adjustment and acceptance of reality.

THE EIGHTIES might be portrayed in blues—swirling aquas, sky blues, and rich royal blues. Simple, uncluttered patterns melt into each other. Overlapping colors and lack of hard edges reflect simplification of life. Angry spots or rectangles can evoke recognition of inevitable losses and health and physical challenges.

THE FUTURE is portrayed in the final block. If a person is aging *beyond* well, it will reflect hope, service, sharing, learning, passion, comforting others, relieving burdens, and creating legacy. These require playful, upbeat colors. The extent to which black, brown, and gray are introduced depends on a person's way of being in the world and their view of the future.

Blocks in a quilt can portray events, defining moments, careers, or even people rather than time. Whatever the content, the composition of colors, patterns, intensity, edges, and artwork create the tone of each block. The overall design presents a magical, cohesive whole—a life artfully illustrated.

> After a five-year-old boy told his mother about an elaborate dream, his little sister wanted to have a dream, too. It was unlikely she understood the concept, but she was determined to have her own dream. Her mother asked what she wanted to dream about. The girl's face crinkled in thought as she put a finger to her chin and searched the air with her eyes. Finally, she said, "Pink."

What colors will you dream for your quilt? How would it depict the ebb and flow of your life? What determines the defining moments or critical times you select to include. Will that final block reflect the intention to create legacy, to go *beyond* aging well, and to deliver a good goodbye?

BOOKS BY NIKKI HANNA
Available on Amazon, Kindle, and www.nikkihanna.com

OUT OF IOWA INTO OKLAHOMA
You Can Take the Girl Out of Iowa, but
You Can't Take the Iowa Out of the Girl

CAPTURE LIFE - WRITE A MEMOIR
Create a Life Story—Leave a Legacy

WRITE WHATEVER THE HELL YOU WANT
Finding Joy and Purpose in Writing

RED HEELS AND SMOKIN'
How I Got My Moxie Back

NEAR SEX EXPERIENCES
A Woman in Crescendo, Aging with Bravado

HEY, KIDS, WATCH THIS
Go BEYOND Aging Well

LEADERSHIP SAVVY
How to Become a Stand-Out Leader, Promote Employee
Loyalty, and Build an Energized Workforce

LISTEN UP, WRITER
How Not to Write Like an Amateur—The Path to Authorship

WORKSHOPS AND PRESENTATIONS

LISTEN UP, WRITER
A Series on How NOT to Write Like an Amateur

Find Joy and Purpose in Writing—encourages writers to take a fresh look at why they write and to develop a definition of success that taps into innate talents and that is achievable.

Tap into Craft—The Road to Authorship—reveals common craft mistakes writers make—the ones that shout *amateur.*

Get the Most Out of Revision, Editing, and Proofing—ensures a writer produces work that is impressive enough to compete in the writing marketplace.

Nail the Structure—Beginnings, Endings, and In Between—covers how to write compelling beginnings and endings and how to keep the middle from slumping.

Write with Voice, Style, and Humor—shows writers how to find personal voice and style so their writing stands out from other writers, delights readers, and impresses publishers.

Capture Life through Memoir—Writing the Hard Stuff—shows how to write a captivating life story, how to write about difficult times and flawed characters, how to decide what to put in and what to leave out, and how to print and publish.

Create Compelling Nonfiction—covers writing principles that apply to various categories of nonfiction (biography/memoir, instructional, self-help, essay, inspirational, illustrative). Writing tips that apply to other genres and publishing options are included.

Apply Winning Strategies to Writing Contests—demonstrates how to be more competitive in contests and how to strategically select them. Key tips increase the odds of winning.

Evaluate Printing, Publishing, and Marketing Options—discloses nuances of the industry and describes the pros and cons of various publishing strategies so writers can make sound, informed decisions.

neqhanna@sbcglobal.net - www.nikkihanna.com

ABOUT THE AUTHOR

When asked to describe herself in one sentence, Nikki Hanna said, "I'm a metropolitan gal who never quite reached the level of refinement and sophistication that label implies." The contradictions reflected in this description are the basis for much of her humorous prose. She describes her writing as irreverent and quirky with strong messages.

As an author, writing coach, and writing contest judge, Hanna is dedicated to inspiring others. She speaks on writing and offers writing workshops on the craft of writing, memoir writing, writing contest strategy, writing with voice/style/humor, finding joy and purpose in writing, and other writing topics. She also speaks on aging, leadership, and women's issues.

In addition to numerous awards for poetry, essays, books, and short stories, Hanna received the Oklahoma Writers' Federation's *Crème de la Crème* Award and Rose State College's Outstanding Writer Award. As a self-published writer, her book awards include the National Indie Excellence Award, the USA Best Book Finalist Award, two international Book Excellence Awards, four Independent Book Awards, and an IPPY (Independent Publisher Book Awards). Her books are available on Amazon and through her website.

Hanna has a BS Degree in Business Education and Journalism and an MBA from The University of Tulsa. A retired CPA and Toastmaster, her years of experience in management and as an executive for one of the country's largest companies fostered a firm grip on leadership. She also served as a consultant on national industry task forces, as a board member for corporations, and as an advisor on curriculum development and strategic planning for educational institutions and charity organizations.

Hanna lives in Tulsa, Oklahoma. She has three children who have decided she had become a bit of a pistol in her old age. Four grandchildren consider her the toy fairy, and those in California believe she lives at the airport.

neqhanna@sbcglobal.net
www.nikkihanna.com

www.ingramcontent.com/pod-product-compliance
Lightning Source LLC
Chambersburg PA
CBHW060745050426
42449CB00008B/1306